A Guide for Protecting Workers from Woodworking Hazards

Small Business Safety Management Series

U.S. Department of Labor
Occupational Safety and Health Administration

OSHA 3157
1999

Contents (continued)

Machines used in woodworking are dangerous, particularly when used improperly or without proper safeguards. Workers operating woodworking equipment suffer the following common injuries: laceration, amputation, severed fingers, and blindness. Wood dust and the chemicals used in finishing are health hazards, and workers in this industry can suffer from skin and respiratory diseases.

The purpose of this guide is to help employers provide a safe and healthful workplace. The guide describes the principal hazards of woodworking and the methods for controlling these hazards. The guide is not a substitute for Occupational Safety and Health Administration (OSHA) standards related to woodworking, but can help clarify the regulatory language and technical information covered in those standards. For more comprehensive information, consult the General Industry Standards, *Title 29 Code of Federal Regulations (CFR), Part 1910*. In particular, Subpart O of the General Industry Standards establishes specific machinery and machine guarding requirements for much of the equipment discussed in this guide. Specific OSHA standards for woodworking are listed in Appendix A of this guide.

Who Should Read This Guide?

If you employ one or more persons to operate woodworking equipment, you should read this guide. This includes employers in industries making wood furniture (household, office, public, and restaurant); wood office and store fixtures; kitchen cabinets and bathroom vanities; industrial patterns; wood containers; wooden musical instruments and toys; and other wood products. Employers at fabricated wood millwork establishments (e.g., establishments that produce doors, windows, porches, and shutters) are also included. This guide does not cover logging operations or the production of lumber and basic wood materials at pulp, paper, or saw mills.

There are many safety and health hazards associated with the above industries. This guide focuses primarily on the safety hazards associated with woodworking machinery and the health hazards of wood dust.

How Will This Guide Help Protect My Employees?

This guide will familiarize you with the hazards of woodworking and the control options for protecting your employees from these hazards. Employing the recommended controls can help you prevent workplace injuries.

This guide also will help you comply with OSHA standards related to woodworking. OSHA regulations require you to protect your employees from workplace hazards caused by machines and hazards associated with the processed material (wood).

What Standards Cover Woodworking?

OSHA has specific standards covering woodworking equipment plus other general regulations that address hazards common to woodworking facilities. This publication primarily covers the regulations for woodworking equipment. A list of the general OSHA regulations covering hazards common to woodworking facilities is included in Appendix A.

Standards for Woodworking Machinery

- General Requirements for All Machines, 29 CFR 1910.212
- Woodworking Machinery Requirements, 29 CFR 1910.213
- Mechanical Power Transmission Apparatus, 29 CFR 1910.219
- Standard for the Prevention of Fires and Explosions in Wood Processing and Woodworking Facilities, NFPA 644-1993
- Woodworking Machinery—Safety Requirements, ANSI O1.1-1992

For a detailed list of other OSHA standards that may apply to the woodworking industry, see Appendix A.

In this document, "shall" and "must" are used to indicate when a control device or other safeguard is required by OSHA; "should" is used to indicate recommended safe work practices.

What Are the Main Types of Hazards Associated with Woodworking Operations?

The principal hazards of woodworking can be classified as either safety or health hazards. **Safety hazards** can cause immediate injury to a worker. For example, if not properly grounded, the metal framework of a circular saw could become energized and possibly electrocute an employee. Or, if a worker's hands were to contact a saw blade, he or she could have one or more fingers cut off.

Safety Hazards

- Machine hazards
  - Point of operation
  - Rotary and reciprocating movements
  - In-running nip points (pinch points)
- Kickbacks
- Flying chips, material
- Tool projection
- Fire and explosion hazards
- Electrical hazards

Most **health hazards** are associated with long-term exposure to certain substances or to excessive noise levels or vibrations. Certain types of wood dust, for example, can cause allergic reactions, and saw dust has been determined to be a group A carcinogen by the International Agency for Research on Cancer (IARC). Likewise, some finishes and coatings used in finishing processes contain chemicals that can affect the central nervous system, causing headaches, nausea, and dizziness. Health hazards can cause both immediate (acute) and longer-term (chronic) health effects. For example, exposure to turpentine, a chemical used in some furniture waxes and finishes, can result in a range of health effects, from temporary irritation of the eyes and skin to kidney and bladder damage.

Health Hazards

- Noise
- Vibration
- Wood dust—carcinogens
- Chemical hazards—from exposure to coatings, finishings, adhesives, solvent vapors

This manual primarily focuses on machine guarding (safety) and wood dust (health) hazards and their controls; however, all of the safety and health topics listed above are addressed.

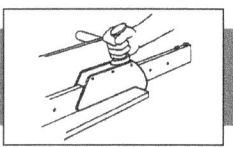
How Can My Employees Recognize the Hazards of Woodworking Equipment?

It is important to train/teach your employees how to identify hazards related to their assigned job tasks. This section provides an overview of the major safety hazards associated with woodworking equipment. The section "Specific Woodworking Equipment Hazards and Controls" covers in more detail each of these hazards and discusses recommended controls for specific types of machinery typically used in woodworking operations.

Point of Operation

The point of operation is the place where work is performed on the material. This is where the stock is cut, shaped, bored, or formed. Most woodworking machines use a cutting and/or shearing action. Table 1 lists examples of how injuries can occur at the point of operation.

Rotating and Reciprocating Movements

All machines operate by rotating or reciprocating motion or by a combination of these motions. For example, rotary cutting and shearing mechanisms, rotating wood stock, flywheels, shaft ends, and spindles all rotate. Rotating action is hazardous regardless of the speed, size, or surface finish of the moving part. Rotating parts and shafts, such as stock projecting from the chuck of a lathe, can catch hair or clothing and draw the operator in. This can seriously mangle or crush the operator. Rotating parts and stock can also force an arm or hand into a dangerous position, breaking bones and lacerating or severing a hand or other parts of a limb. Bolts, projecting keys, or screws on rotating parts increase the danger of getting caught by the rotary part. Operators can also be struck by a projecting bolt or key.

Table 1.
How Do Injuries Occur at the Point of Operation?

- Employees can be injured if their hands get too close to the blade, particularly when working on small pieces of stock. The size of the piece dictates that the operator's hand be close to the blade. Accidents can occur when stock unexpectedly moves or when a worker's hand slips.

- Stock can get stuck in a blade and actually pull the operator's hands into the machine.

- Employees can be injured if the machine or its guard is not properly adjusted or maintained. An improperly adjusted radial saw, for example, might not return to its starting position after making a cut.

- If the machine has controls that are not recessed or remote, and the equipment is accidentally started, a worker's hands may be caught at the point of operation.

- Contact also can occur during machine repair or cleaning if care is not taken to de-energize the machine—that is, if lockout/tagout procedures are not followed.

- An employee may be injured if he or she reaches in to clean a saw or remove a piece of wood after the saw has been turned off, but is still coasting or idling. Also, saw blades often move so fast that it can be difficult to determine whether they are moving. This is especially a problem under fluorescent lighting.

Reciprocating movement is back-and-forth or up-and-down motion. Operators can be caught and crushed by reciprocating movement when the moving part approaches or crosses a fixed part of the machine. (See Figure 1.)

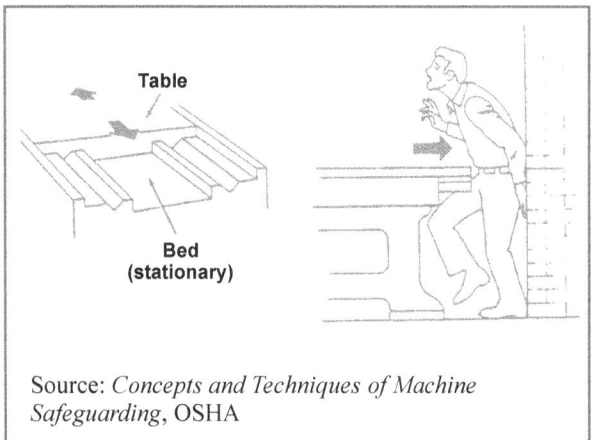

Source: *Concepts and Techniques of Machine Safeguarding*, OSHA

Figure 1. Reciprocating Movement

In-Running Nip Points

In-running nip points (or pinch points) are a special danger arising from rotating or reciprocating parts. They occur whenever machine parts move toward each other or when one part moves past a stationary object. Parts of the body may be caught between or drawn into the nip point and crushed, mangled, or severed. Figure 2 shows some in-running nip points that may be encountered in the woodworking industry. The nip points in this figure are located where the belts or chains approach the pulleys or gears, or where the rotating parts approach the stationary components.

Kickbacks

Kickbacks occur when a saw seizes the stock and hurls it back at the operator. This can happen when the stock twists and binds against the side of the blades or is caught in the teeth. A blade that is not sharpened, or that is set at an incorrect height, can cause kickbacks. Poor-quality lumber (in other words, frozen lumber or lumber with many knots or foreign objects such as nails) can also result in kickbacks. Hazards due to kickbacks are most likely when there is a lack of safeguards, such as spreaders, anti-kickback fingers, and gauge or rip

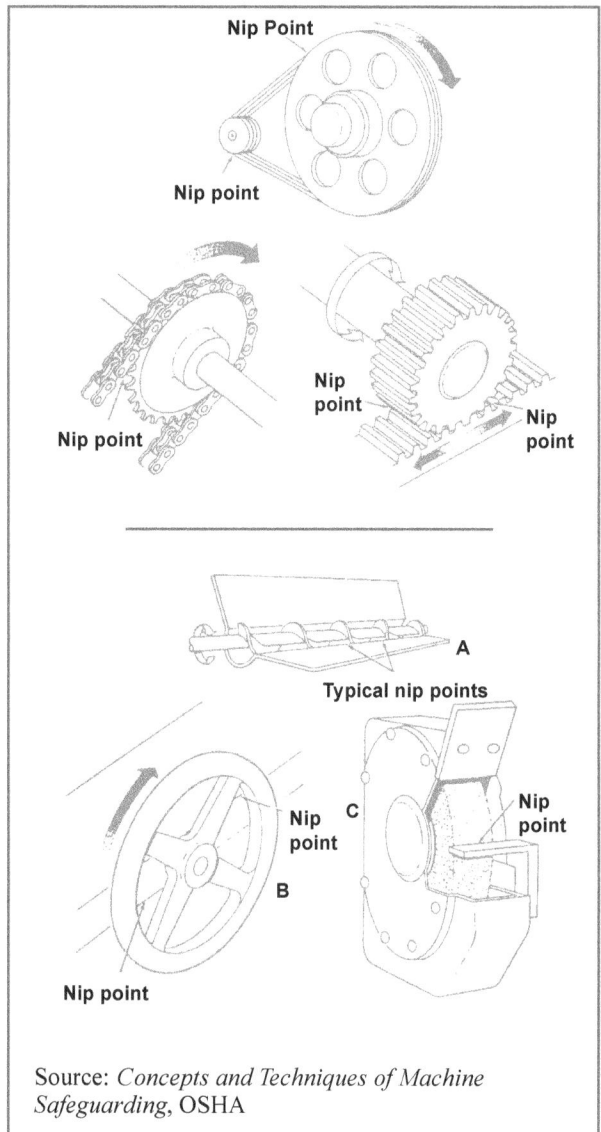

Source: *Concepts and Techniques of Machine Safeguarding*, OSHA

Figure 2. In-Running Nip Points

fences. Kickbacks occur more often when cutting parallel to the wood grain (ripping) than when cross-cutting.

Flying Chips

Employees may be exposed to splinters and chips that are flung by the cutting action of woodworking equipment.

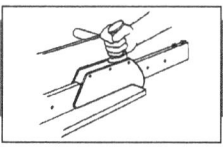
Tool Projection (Unbalanced Cutter Heads)

Many pieces of woodworking equipment—such as routers, shapers, and molders—employ rotating cutter heads with multiple knives. Cutter heads that are not properly adjusted, or that are poorly mounted or have broken knives, can become unbalanced. Balance is critical for keeping knives secured to a rapidly moving cutter head. The centrifugal forces on an unbalanced cutter head can fling the knives from the tool and severely or fatally injure the operator or other nearby personnel. Using the wrong tool on a cutter head or using a tool at a higher speed than it was designed to operate at also can cause tool breakage and projection.

What Controls Are Available to Help Protect My Employees from Machine Hazards?

The preferred way to control hazards is through engineering or work practice controls. When these controls are not possible or do not provide adequate protection, personal protective equipment (PPE) must be provided as a supplement. Employers must institute all feasible engineering and work practice controls to eliminate or reduce hazards before using PPE to protect employees.

Engineering controls involve physically changing the machine or work environment to prevent employee exposure to the potential hazard. Examples are using a guard on a machine, or using local exhaust ventilation to remove dust and other contaminants at the source.

Work practice controls involve removing your employees from exposure to the potential hazard by changing the way they do their jobs. For example, workers should always use push sticks to guide short or narrow pieces of stock through saws. Using a push stick allows saw operators to keep their hands at a safe distance from the saw blades. (See Figure 3.)

Router Operator Killed by Flying Tool

A 32-year-old experienced woodworker was fatally injured at work while operating an overarm router. The worker was making custom rosettes when a steel tool knife was propelled from the rosette cutter. The knife penetrated a Plexiglas shield, and then penetrated and exited his chest. The knife ricocheted off a wall before landing.

The knife, measuring approximately 1 5/8 inches square, was part of a cutter-head assembly that had been previously used on a drill press at much lower cutting speeds. It was custom designed for the drill press, not for the router, which is run at much higher speeds. The knife was held in the cutter head by flat shims and set screws; the screws could not counteract the centrifugal forces generated by the high-speed rotation.

Fatality Investigation Report 2:2, February 1997, Occupational Health Surveillance Program, Massachusetts Department of Public Health.

Source: *Accident Prevention Manual for Industrial Operations*, National Safety Council

Figure 3. Push Stick Work Practice Control

Personal protective equipment encompasses a wide variety of devices and garments designed to protect workers from injuries. Examples include respirators, goggles, safety shields, hard hats, gloves, earmuffs, and earplugs.

What Engineering Controls Are Available to Help Protect My Employees from Machine Hazards?

Machine Guarding

Guards are now standard equipment on most woodworking machines. If you purchase a machine that does not come equipped with a guard, install one. Contact the manufacturer of the machine to see if appropriate guard(s) are available for the equipment. If not, use this guide to help you determine the appropriate guard to install. Because woodworking equipment is dangerous, guards should always be designed and installed by technically competent and qualified persons. In addition, it is always a good idea to have the equipment manufacturer review proposed guard designs to ensure that the guard will adequately protect employees and allow safe operation of the equipment.

There are many ways to guard machines. The type of operation, size or shape of stock, work being performed on the material, method of handling, and production requirements are some of the factors that help determine the appropriate safeguarding method for an individual machine. All moving machine parts that may cause injury must be safeguarded. This includes the point of operation, the power transmission apparatus, and rotary or reciprocating parts. Table 2 describes three types of machine guards commonly used on woodworking machinery: fixed, adjustable, and self-adjusting.

To be effective, a guard should prevent employees from contacting the dangerous parts of the machines, and it should be secure. This is not always possible, as in the case of the radial arm saw. Regardless, workers should not be able to easily bypass, remove, or otherwise tamper with the guard. In protecting the worker, however, the guard must not create additional hazards, nor prevent the worker from performing the job.

Make sure that guards are in working order and that they are appropriate and practical for the machinery. Guards must have adequate strength to resist blows and strains and should be constructed to protect operators from flying splinters and

machine parts such as broken saw teeth, cutting heads, and tools.

For more information on methods of machine guarding (including construction of guards), consult Appendix A of this guide. The section "Specific Woodworking Equipment Hazards and Controls" provides more detailed information on guard types for specific woodworking machines.

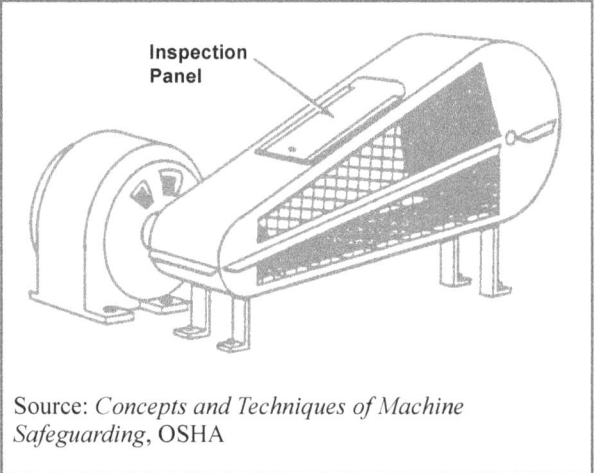

Source: *Concepts and Techniques of Machine Safeguarding*, OSHA

Figure 4. Fixed Guard on Belt and Pulley

Source: *Health and Safety Guide for Wooden Furniture Manufacturing*, NIOSH

Figure 5. Fixed Guard on Planer

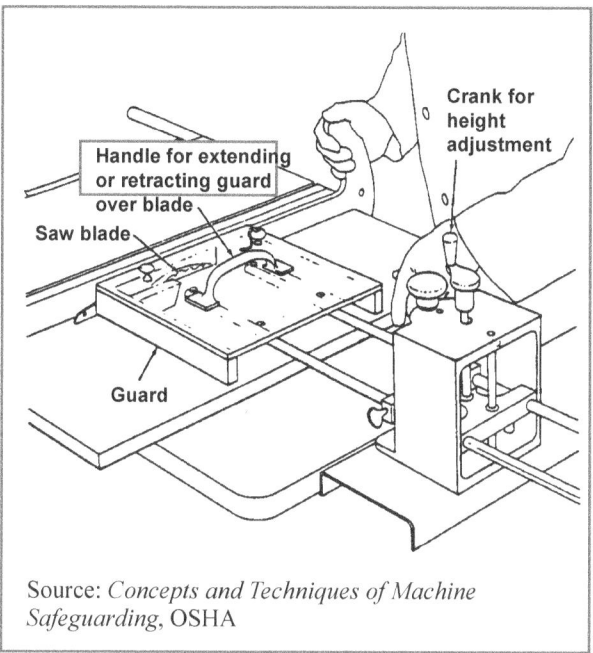

Source: *Concepts and Techniques of Machine Safeguarding*, OSHA

Figure 6. Adjustable Guard on Table Saw

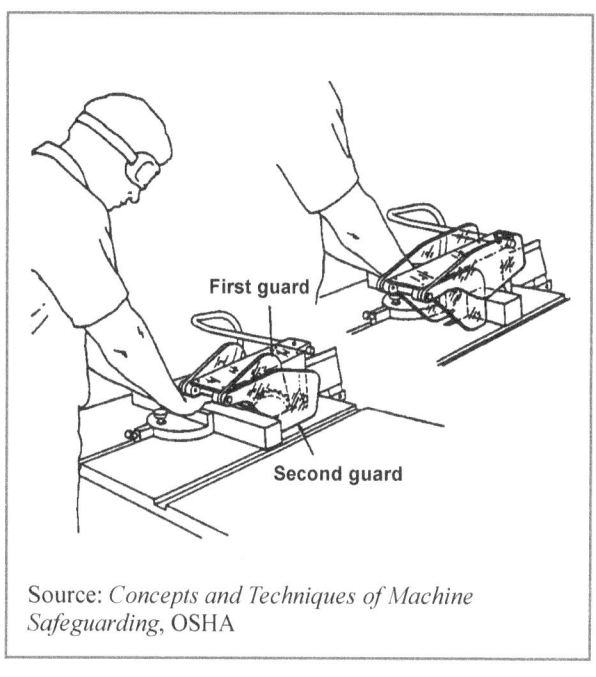

Source: *Concepts and Techniques of Machine Safeguarding*, OSHA

Figure 8. Self-Adjusting Guard on Table Saw

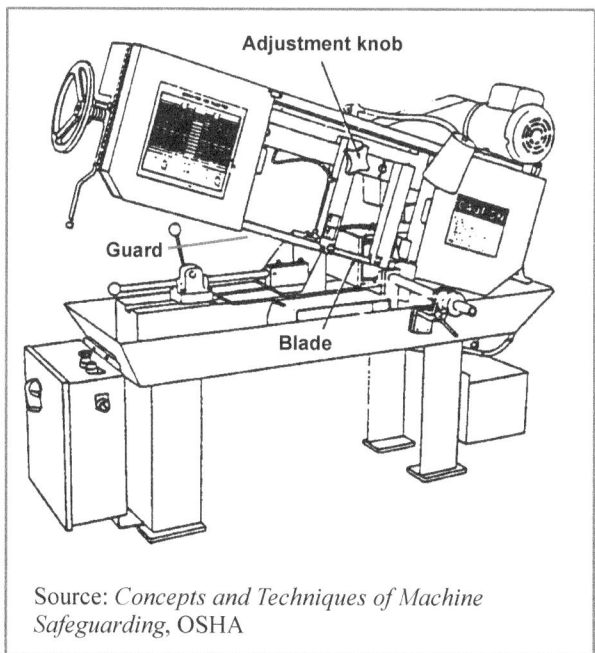

Source: *Concepts and Techniques of Machine Safeguarding*, OSHA

Figure 7. Adjustable Guard on Horizontal Band Saw

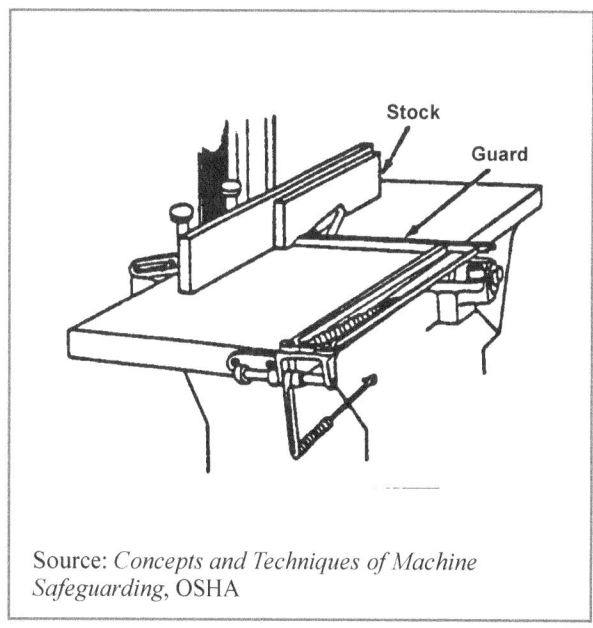

Source: *Concepts and Techniques of Machine Safeguarding*, OSHA

Figure 9. Self-Adjusting Guard on Jointer

Table 2. Types of Machine Guards

		Types of Machine Guards		
Type	Safeguarding Action	Advantages	Limitations	Examples
Fixed	Provides a barrier and is a permanent part of machine.	• Can be constructed to suit many specific applications. • Can provide maximum protection. • Usually requires little maintenance. • Suitable to high production, repetitive operations.	• May interfere with visibility. • Machine adjustment and repair often require removal of guard. • Other means of protecting maintenance personnel often required (i.e., lockout).	Use on: • In-running rolls. • Belts and pulleys (see Figure 4). • Power transmission apparatus. • Cutting heads of planers and other automatic-feed equipment (see Figure 5).
Adjustable	Provides a barrier that may be adjusted to facilitate a variety of production operations.	• Can be constructed to suit many specific applications. • Can be adjusted to admit varying sizes of stock.	• Hands may enter danger area protection may not be complete at all times. • May require frequent maintenance or adjustment. • Operator may make guard ineffective. • May interfere with visibility.	Used on woodworking machinery, such as: • Table saws (see Figure 6). • Routers. • Shapers. • Band saws (see Figure 7).
Self-adjusting	Provides a barrier that moves according to the size of the stock entering the point of operation. Guard is in place when machine is at rest. Guard pushes away when worker moves stock into point of operation.	• Off-the-shelf guards are often commercially available. • Do not require manual adjustments.	• Does not provide maximum protection. • May interfere with visibility. • May require frequent maintenance and adjustment.	Used on woodworking machinery, such as: • Table saws (see Figure 8). • Radial saws. • Band saws. • Jointers (see Figure 16).

Source: Adapted from *Concepts and Techniques of Machine Safeguarding*, U.S. Department of Labor, OSHA.

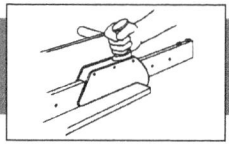
Other Means of Safeguarding Machines

Additional methods for safeguarding machines include guarding by location or distance, feeding methods, and appropriate placement of controls. None of these methods should replace machine guards, however. It is always important to provide a guard or barrier that prevents access to the danger area. Table 3 describes these other safeguarding methods.

Table 3. Other Methods of Safeguarding Machines

Other Methods of Safeguarding Machines			
Method	**Safeguarding Principle**	**Examples**	**Comments**
Location/distance	Dangerous parts of machinery positioned so that they are not accessible to workers during normal operation.	• Placement of machine's power apparatus against wall. • Fencing off access to automatic machines. • Feeding long stock into machine.	Not always feasible, particularly on non-automatic machines.
Automatic Feeding and Ejection Methods	Operator not required to place his or her hands in the danger area.	• Self-feeder planers. • Sanders. • Lathes.	Malfunctioning can create hazard. Controls should be set at a distance.
Prevent Accidental Startup	Controls shrouded or recessed.	Standard on many machines.	Off switch should be easily accessible, and operator should be able to operate machine with ease.
Miscellaneous	Hazardous part of machine automatically retracted after operation is complete.	Counterweight/stroking mechanisms that return blade to rest after stock has been cut on overhead swing and radial saws.	Improperly adjusted counterweights can create hazard. Blade may travel in wrong direction or may fail to retract.
Placement of Controls	Place controls sufficiently far from point of operation to prevent reaching into point of operation.	Two hand controls sit at a distance from the point of operation.	Stopping time of machine is a factor in calculating the distance.

Source: *Accident Prevention Manual for Industrial Operations*, National Safety Council

What Procedural and Administrative Controls Are Needed to Protect Employees from Equipment Hazards?

• **Use appropriate equipment for the job**. Workers can be seriously injured if they do not use the correct equipment for a job. Use machines only for work within the rated capacity specified by the machine manufacturer. Use the correct tools on a given machine. For example, when using a circular saw, use the correct blade for the required cutting action. Similarly, you must only mount blades, cutter heads, or collars on machine arbors that have been accurately sized and shaped to fit these parts.

• **Train workers on machine use and allow only trained and authorized workers to operate and maintain the equipment**. Workers should understand the purpose and function of all controls on the machine, should know how to stop the equipment in an emergency, and should be trained on the safety procedures for special set-ups.

Operator training should include hazards associated with the machine, how the safeguards protect the worker from these hazards, under what circumstances the guard may be removed (usually just for maintenance), and what to do if the guard is damaged or not functioning properly.

Employees should be able to demonstrate their ability to run the machine with all safety precautions and mechanisms in place.

• **Frequently inspect equipment and guards.** Ensure that: (1) the operator and machine are equipped with the safety accessories suitable for the hazards of the job, (2) the machine and safety equipment are in proper working condition, and (3) the machine operator is properly trained. Document the inspections and keep the records. Documentation should identify the machine, inspection date, problems noted, and corrective action taken. Noting problems helps to ensure that corrective action will be taken, that operators on all shifts will be made aware of

any potential danger, and that any pattern of repeat problems on a particular machine can be detected and resolved as early as possible.

• **Use equipment only when guards are in place and in working order**. A worker should not be allowed to operate a piece of woodworking equipment if the guard or any other safety device, return device, spreader, anti-kickback fingers apparatus, guard on in-running rolls, or gauge or rip fence is not functioning properly. When guards cannot be used (during rabbeting or dadoing, for instance), you must provide combs, featherboards, or suitable jigs for holding the stock.

• **You must provide your employees with push sticks or other hand tools so that their hands are away from the point of operation when they work on small pieces of stock.** A push stick is a strip of wood or block with a notch cut into one end that is used to push short or narrow lengths of material through saws. (See Figure 10.) Using push sticks keeps stock from tipping and prevents the operator's fingers from coming in contact with blades.

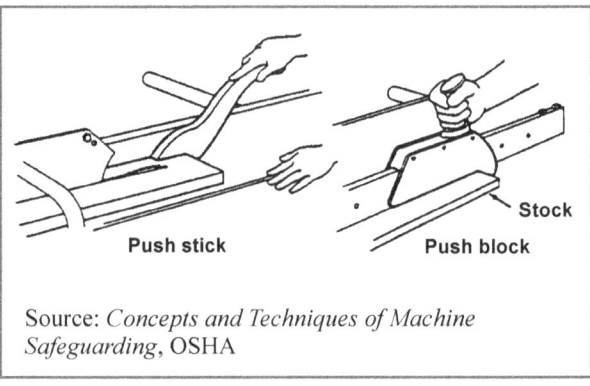

Source: *Concepts and Techniques of Machine Safeguarding*, OSHA

Figure 10. Push Stick and Push Block

• **Use a brush or stick to clean sawdust and scrap from a machine**. Never allow your employees to clean a saw with their hands or while the machine is running.

• **Provide regular preventive maintenance**. Regularly clean and maintain woodworking equipment and guards. Ensure that blades are in good condition. Knives and cutting heads must

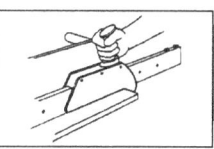
be kept sharp, properly adjusted, and secured. Sharpening blades prevents kickback. You must also remove any cracked or damaged blades from service. Keep circular saw blades round and balanced. You must remove dull, badly set, improperly filed or improperly tensioned saws from service, and immediately clean saws to which gum has adhered.

- **Never leave a machine unattended in the "on" position**. Make sure that workers know never to leave a machine that has been turned off but is still coasting.

- **Maintain proper housekeeping**. Workers have been injured by tripping and then falling onto the blades of saws. You must keep floors and aisles in good repair and free from debris, dust, protruding nails, unevenness, or other tripping hazards. Do not use compressed air to blow away chips and debris. Make sure you have a non-slip floor.

- **Do not allow workers to wear loose clothing or long hair**. Loose clothing or long hair can be easily caught up in rotating parts.

- **Never saw freehand. Always hold the stock against a gauge or fence**. Freehand sawing increases the likelihood of an operator's hands coming in contact with the blade.

- See the "Personal Protective Equipment" section, located near the end of this guide, for a discussion of PPE.

- Use appropriate personal protective equipment. See the "Personal Protective Equipment" section of this guide for additional information.

This section covers the major safety hazards of specific woodworking machinery, and discusses the engineering controls and work procedures for minimizing employee exposure to these hazards. References to applicable OSHA standards are provided in the text of this section in cases where the engineering controls or work practices are required by a specific OSHA standard. Note that not all OSHA requirements are covered in this section. Consult OSHA's woodworking machinery standard [29 CFR 1910.213] to ensure that you are in compliance with all requirements.

Personal protective equipment is not covered in this section because the same recommendations discussed in the "Personal Protective Equipment" section of this guide apply to all machinery.[1] Similarly, work practices that apply to all woodworking equipment (such as using a brush for cleaning saws) are not covered here.

Circular/Crosscut/Ripsaws

These table saws are used for straight sawing. Depending on the blade, they cut either across (crosscut) or with (ripsaw) the grain of the wood. With the hand-fed saws, the operator adjusts the height and angle of the blade. Then, holding the stock, the operator pushes it into the blade. A guide is used to maintain a straight cut at the desired width. At the end of the cutting stroke, the operator either changes positions or pushes the stock past the blade. Self-feed or power table saws are equipped with rollers or a conveyor system to hold the lumber and force-feed it into the saw blade.

Injuries can occur if an operator's hands slip as he or she is feeding the stock into the saw or if the operator holds his or her hands too close to the blades while cutting. Employees can also be injured when removing scrap or finished pieces from the table. Kickbacks (that is, when the blade catches the stock and throws it back toward the operator) are another major cause of injury. Kickbacks can result if the blade height is not correct or if the blade is not properly maintained. Kickbacks are more likely to occur when ripping, rather than crosscutting. Kickbacks also can occur if safeguards are not used or if poor-quality lumber is cut.

Safety Hazards of Circular/Crosscut/Ripsaws

- Point of operation—Contact with the turning blade may occur.

- Other moving parts—Contact with the blade under the table, or with the power transmission apparatus (if not enclosed), may occur.

- Kickbacks—Stock caught by the blade may be thrown back at the operator.

- Flying particles—Wood chips, splinters, and broken saw teeth may be thrown by the cutting action of the blade.

- Nip points from automatic feed—Clothing, hair, or hands may be caught by and pulled into the in-running rolls.

Engineering Controls

- Ripsaws and crosscut saws. Enclose the portion of the saw above the table with a self- adjusting guard, as shown in Figure 11. The guard must adjust to the thickness of the material being cut and remain in contact with it [29 CFR 1910.213 (c)(1) and (d)(1)]. Hinge the guard so that the blades can be easily changed.

- For ripsaws, use a spreader to prevent material from squeezing the saw or kicking back during ripping [29 CFR 1910.213(c)(2)]. Use anti-kickback fingers to hold the stock down in the event that the saw kicks back the material [29 CFR 1910.213(c)(3)].

- Guard all belts and in-running nip points [29 CFR 1910.212(a)(1), 1910.219(d) and (e)].

- Always guard the portion of the blade below the table. Operators must be protected from possible contact when reaching under the table [29 CFR 1910.213(a)(12)].

---

[1] For further information on personal protective equipment, please consult OSHA publication #3151, entitled *Assessing the Need for Personal Protective Equipment: A Guide for Small Business Employers.*

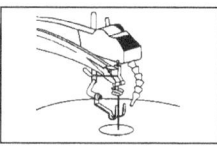
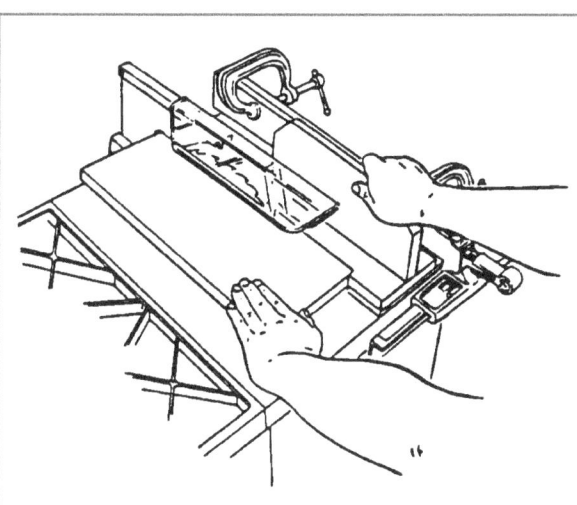

Source: *Accident Prevention Manual for Industrial Operations*, National Safety Council

Figure 11. Saw Blade with a Self-Adjusting Guard

- Attach a brake to the motor's arbor to stop the saw from coasting after it has been cut off, or have the operator remain at the saw station once the motor is shut off until the blade stops turning.

- Guard feed rolls on self feed circular saws by a hood or guard to prevent hands from coming into contact with in-running rip points [1910.213(f)(1)].

Work Procedures

- Keep hands out of the line of the cut.
- Use proper blade for cutting action (for example, don't use crosscut blade for ripping).
- Operate saw at speed specified by the manufacturer.
- Maintain and sharpen blade [1910.213(s)(2)].
- Leave sufficient clearance for stock.
- Remove cracked saws from service [29 CFR 1910.213(s)(7)].
- Stand to side of the saw blade to avoid injury due to kickback.
- Guide stock parallel to the rip fence to minimize the potential for kickback.

- Use a push stick for small pieces of wood and for pushing stock past the blade. [1910.213(s)(9)]

- Avoid crosscutting long boards on table saws. Considerable hand pressure is required close to the saw blade, and the boards create a safety hazard to other people.

- Use a filler piece between the fence and the saw blade when necessary (e.g., when there is little clearance on the fence side).

- Properly support all pieces of stock, including the cut and uncut ends, scrap, and finished product.

Overhead Swing and Straight Line Pull Cutoff Saws

These are special types of circular saws, which are also used for straight cutting. They are preferred for cutting long pieces of stock. The overhead swing saw is suspended from the ceiling, as shown in Figure 12; the saw is generally attached directly to the motor shaft. To run the saw the operator pulls it forward like a pendulum.

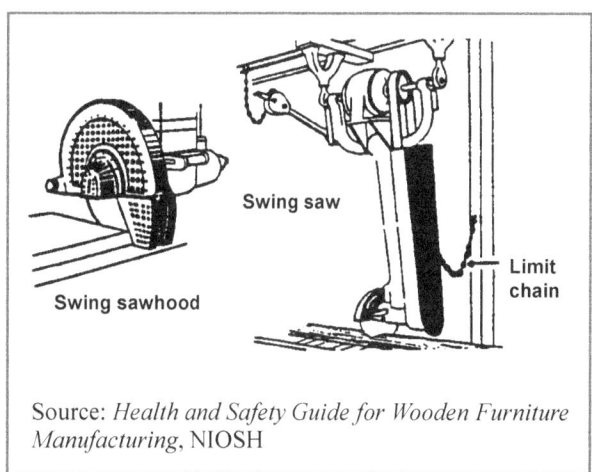

Source: *Health and Safety Guide for Wooden Furniture Manufacturing*, NIOSH

Figure 12. Overhead Swing Saw

Injuries can occur if the operator reaches to remove a section of board while the blade is coasting or idling, or if the operator tries to measure a board or position it while the saw is still running. Injuries can also occur if an improperly adjusted saw swings beyond its safe limits.

> ### Safety Hazards of Overhead Swing and Straight Line Pull Cutoff Saws
>
> • Point of operation—Contact with the blade may occur during operation, when the saw is idling; if the return device fails, or if the saw bounces forward from a retracted position.
>
> • In-running nip points—Clothing, hair, or hands may be caught by and pulled into the in- running rolls of automatic feed.
>
> • Kickback—Stock caught by the blade may be thrown back at the operator.
>
> • Flying particles—Wood chips, splinters, and broken saw teeth may be thrown by the cutting action of the blade.

Engineering Controls

• Enclose upper half of saw and arbor end with a fixed guard; enclose the point of operation (the lower part of the blade) with a self-adjusting hood. The hood must drop on top of and remain in contact with the table or stock. When the saw returns to the back of the table, the hood must cover the lower portion of the blade [29 CFR 1910.213(g)(1)].

• Ensure that the saw contains an automatic device (for example, a counterweight) to return the saw to the back of the table after the cut has been made [29 CFR 1910.213(g)(2)].

• Install a latch with a rachet release on the handle, nonrecoil spring, bumper, or other device to keep the saw from rebounding from its idle position.

• Use limit chains or other means to keep saw from moving beyond the front or back edge of the table [29 CFR 1910.213(g)(3)]. (See Figure 12.)

• Enclose overhead drive with a fixed guard [29 CFR 1910.219].

Work Practices

• Position the piece to be cut before starting the saw.

• Stand at the side of the saw blade when the saw is running, and use the hand nearest the handle to operate the saw. (This keeps the operator's body out of the line of the saw.)

• Remove cracked and defective saw blades from service [29 CFR 1910.213(s)(7)].

• Keep hands out of the line of the cut.

• Make sure guards and counterweights are properly adjusted at all times. Take improperly adjusted saws out of service [29 CFR 1910.213 (s)(1)].

Radial Saws

Radial saws are circular saws that cut downward, either with or against the wood grain (rip or crosscut). For crosscutting, the wood is pushed away from the operator and against a fence. For rip cuts, the blade is set parallel to the fence, and the stock is pushed through. The saw blade rotates upward toward the operator; who feeds the stock in the opposite direction of the blade movement.

Radial saws have features that make them more versatile than table saws. The saw arm can be raised and lowered and swung from side to side to adjust the depth and horizontal angle of the cut; the blade can be replaced with shaping cutters, disk or drum sanders, and other accessories.

The principal types of injury from radial saws are cuts to the arms and hands, or amputation of fingers, from contact with the blade or flying wood chips. Workers can also be injured from kickback. Employees working nearby can be seriously injured if stock that is fed in the wrong direction is flung out of the saw.

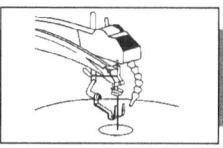
Engineering Controls

- Enclose the upper half of the saw (from the blade down to the end of the saw arbor) with a fixed hood. Guard the lower half with a self-adjusting, floating guard that rises and falls and automatically adjusts to the thickness of the stock [29 CFR 1910.213(h)(1)]. Figure 13 shows a radial saw with a self-adjusting guard covering the lower half of the blade.

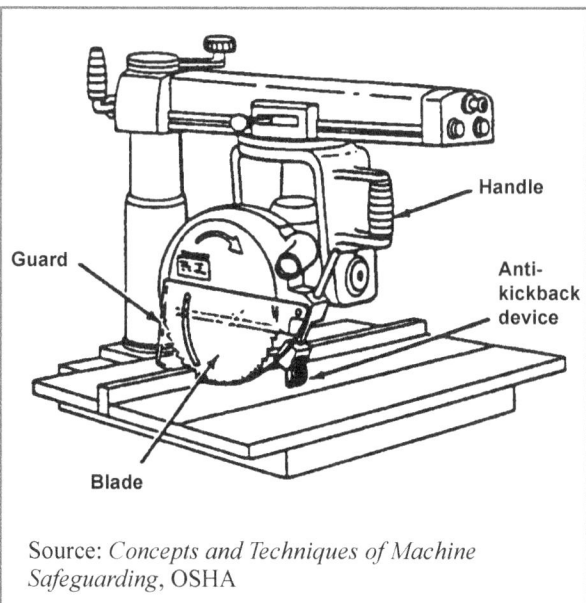

Source: *Concepts and Techniques of Machine Safeguarding*, OSHA

Figure 13. Radial Saw with Self-Adjusting Guard

- Make sure the saw has a return device. The front end of the unit must be slightly higher than the rear, so that the cutting head will return to its original position when released by the operator. This should also prevent the cutting head from rolling or moving the arm due to gravity or vibration [29 CFR 1910.213(h)(4)].

- Install an adjustable stop to limit forward travel distance of the blade during repeat cuts [1910.213(h)(3)].

- Guard feed rolls [29 CFR 1910.213(b)(7)].

- For ripping, install non-kickback fingers on both sides of the saw blade [29 CFR 1910.213(h)(2)].

- Use a spreader in ripping operations to prevent the cut in the wood from immediately closing and binding the blade.

Work Practices

- During crosscutting, operate the saw on the side of table with the handle.

- Make sure that stock is fed in the correct direction. Post a warning label on the hood showing the direction of saw rotation [29 CFR 1910.213(h)(5)].

- Measure boards against a stop gauge, or turn off the saw if measuring by rule. (Wait for the blade to stop before moving materials or making measurements.)

Band Saws

Band saws are used for both straight sawing and for cutting curved pieces. The band saw uses a thin, flexible, continuous steel strip with cutting teeth on one edge. The blade runs on two pulleys, driven and idler, through a hole in the work table on which stock is fed. The operator hand-feeds and manipulates the stock against the blade to saw along a predetermined line.

Although workers are not injured as frequently or as severely on band saws as on circular saws, injuries do occur. The most common injury is caused by contact with the blade. Contact with the blade at the point of operation occurs because the operator's hands may come close to the blade during cutting, and band saws cannot be completely guarded.

Safety Hazards of Band Saws

- Point of operation—Contact with the moving blade may occur.
- In-running nip points—Clothing, hair, or hands may be caught by and pulled into feed rolls or the pulley mechanism.
- Kickbacks—Stock caught by the blade may be thrown back at the operator.
- Flying Chips—Wood chips and splinters may be thrown by the cutting action of the blade.

Engineering Controls

- Guard the blade entirely except at the point of operation (the working portion of the blade between the bottom of the guide rolls and the table) [29 CFR 1910.213(i)(1)]. (See Figure 14.)
- Use a self-adjusting guard for the portion of the blade between the sliding guide and the upper saw so that it raises and lowers with the guide [29 CFR 1910.213(i)(1)].
- Properly adjust the blade guide post to fit the thickness of the stock and to provide additional guarding.
- Fully enclose the pulley mechanism [29 CFR 1910.219(d)].
- Guard feed rolls [29 CFR 1910.213(i)(3)].
- Install a brake on one or both wheels to minimize the potential for coasting after the saw has been shut off; or do not retrieve material until the blade has stopped.
- Make sure the saw includes a tension control device to indicate proper blade tension [29 CFR 1910.213(i)(2)].

Work Procedures

- Use a blade of an appropriate size and type (for example, do not force a wide saw to cut on a small radius).

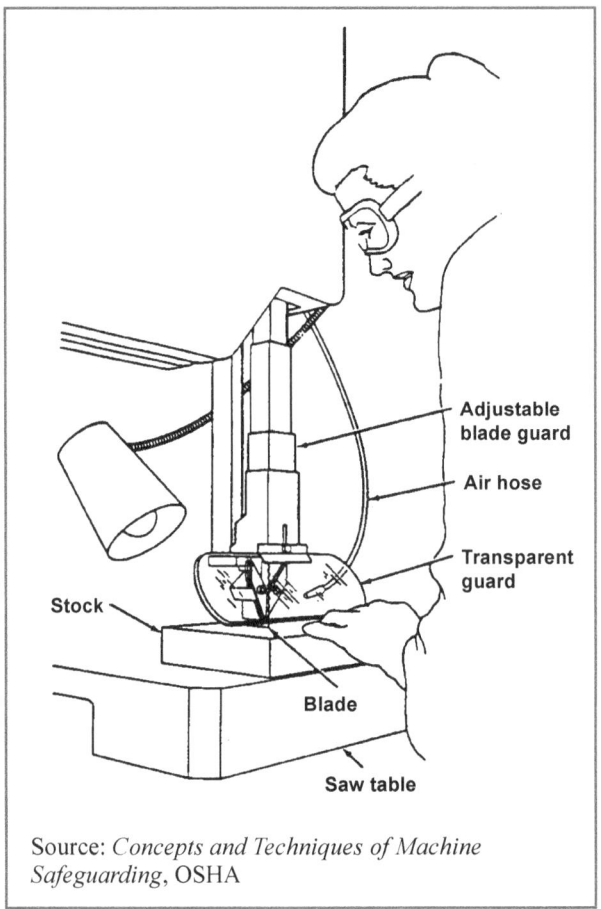

Source: *Concepts and Techniques of Machine Safeguarding*, OSHA

Figure 14. Adjustable Guard on Band Saw

- Never stop the saw too quickly or thrust a piece of wood against the cutting edge of the teeth after the power has been shut off.
- Periodically examine blades; remove cracked or defective blades immediately [29 CFR.1910.213(s)(7)].
- Make cuts only when the power is on and not while the saw is coasting.
- Set the guard to just clear the stock being cut.
- Use a push stick to control the stock when it is near the blade.
- Use a special jig or fixture when cutting small pieces of stock.

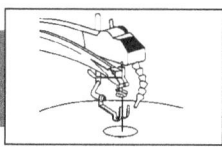
Jig Saws

Jig saws are useful for precision-cutting intricate curves and patterns on thin stock. They have thin blades that move rapidly up and down through the opening in the saw table. The blade is held in upper and lower chucks that pull it tight and keep it from bending. A hold-down adjusts to the thickness of the wood being cut.

Jig saws are generally not considered to be as dangerous as other saws; however, contact at the point of operation can cause hand and finger injuries. Contact with the blade can also occur below the table. All portions of the blade must be guarded.

> ### Safety Hazards of Jig Saws
>
> • Point of operation—Contact with the moving blade may occur.
>
> • In-running nip points—Clothing, hair, or hands may be caught by and pulled into the in-running rolls.
>
> • Flying chips—Wood chips and splinters may be thrown by the cutting action.
>
> • Kickback—Stock caught by the blade may be thrown back at operator.

Engineering Controls

• Use a threshold rest (slotted foot) to hold the stock.

• Guard the blade with an adjustable or self-adjusting guard (see Figure 15).

• Guard drive belts and pulleys [29 CFR 1910.213(a)(9)].

• Guard the portion of the blade below the table.

Work Practices

• Make turns slowly; do not make sharp turns with a wide blade; use a narrow blade for sharp turns.

• Make sure the blade is properly attached and secured.

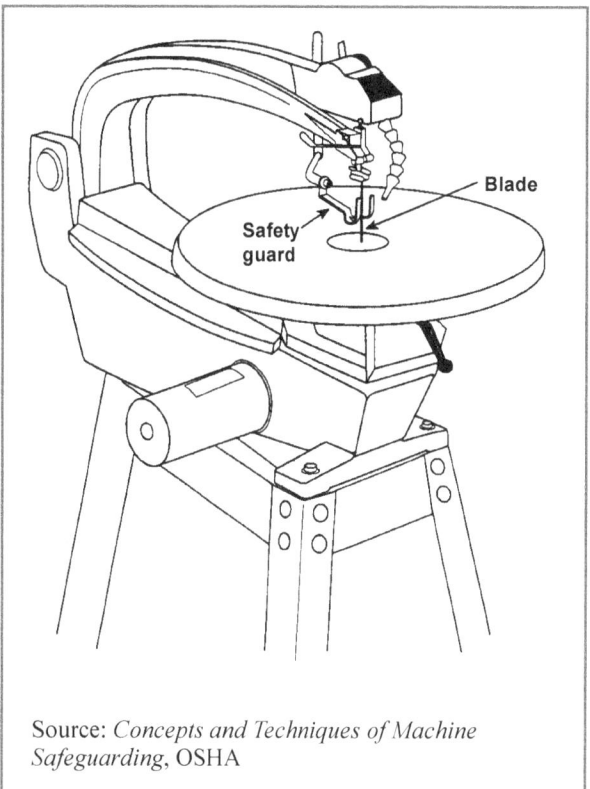

Source: *Concepts and Techniques of Machine Safeguarding*, OSHA

Figure 15. Jig Saw

Jointers

Jointers face or flatten wood and are primarily used to joint small pieces of material. The operator passes stock over a cylindrical, multiple-knife cutter head, while keeping the stock flush against a guide. The depth of the cut is achieved by adjusting the front table. There are two types of jointers: hand-fed jointers with a horizontal cutting head, and wood jointers with a vertical head.

Hand-fed jointers are dangerous woodworking machines. Injuries can occur if the operator's hands and fingers come in contact with the knives. This can happen when the operator is jointing narrow lengths of stock, particularly if he or she does not use a jig or other holding device. Injuries can occur when the operator allows his or her fingers to ride along the surface of the jointer as the wood is fed through. Also, stock may be accidentally kicked away, exposing the operator's hands to the cutter head.

Safety Hazards of Jointers

- Point of operation—Contact with the knives may occur, especially if a holding device is not used.

- In-running nip points—Clothing, hair, or hands may be caught by and pulled into the in- running rolls of the automatic feed.

- Kickbacks—Stock may be thrown back at the operator after being caught by the knives; this may also expose the operator's hands to the knives.

- Flying chips—Wood chips and splinters may be thrown by the cutting action of the knives.

Engineering Controls

For hand-fed jointers, horizontal head:

- Enclose cutter head with an automatic (spring-loaded, self-enclosing) guard that exposes the cutter head only when the stock is being fed. The guard must automatically adjust to cover the unused portion of the head, and it must remain in contact with the material at all times [29 CFR 1910.213(j)(3)]. Figure 16 shows the appropriate use of a self-adjusting guard.

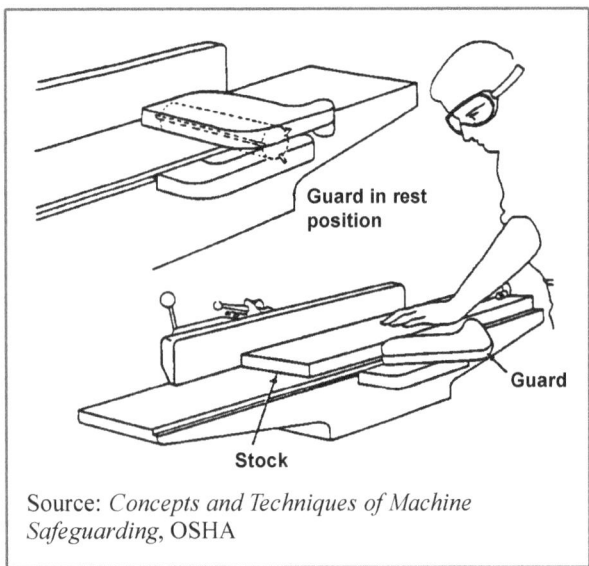

Guard in rest position

Guard

Stock

Source: *Concepts and Techniques of Machine Safeguarding*, OSHA

Figure 16. Jointer with Self-Adjusting Guard

- Adjust the cylindrical cutter head so that the knife projects no more than 1/8 inch beyond the cylindrical body of the head [29 CFR 1910.213(j)(1)].

- Adjust the cutter head so that the clearance between the path of the knife projection and the rear table is no more than 1/8 inch [29 CFR 1910.213(j)(2)].

- Keep the clearance between the table and the head as small as possible [29 CFR 1910.213(j)(2)].

For vertical head jointers:

- Completely enclose cutter head, except for slot to apply the material for jointing. This guard can be part of the local exhaust system.

Work Practices

- Use hold-down push blocks when jointing wood narrower than 3 inches.

- Avoid deep cuts; they increase the likelihood of kickbacks and require a larger table opening.

- As a general rule, never joint pieces of material that are less than four times the width of the bed opening.

- Check knives regularly for proper setting and adjustment, but only when the power is shut off.

Shapers

Shapers are most commonly used to shape the edges of stock. The operator feeds the stock from any direction against a vertical rotating cutter mounted on a spindle. The spindle rotates at a high speed. Some machines have multiple spindles. Guidepins hold the stock for curved shaping and fences hold it for straight line shaping.

Injuries can occur when the operator's hands or fingers contact the revolving knives. Workers can also be seriously injured or killed by tool projection from unbalanced cutter heads. Shapers are difficult to guard; however, a number of guards are available to protect operators' hands.

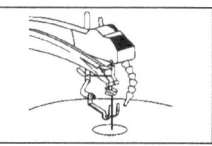
Safety Hazards of Shapers

- Point of operation—Contact with the cutter head may occur, particularly if holding devices are not used.

- Tool projection—Knives may be flung if the cutter head is unbalanced.

- Kickback—Stock may be thrown back at the operator after being caught by the cutter head.

- Flying chips—Wood chips and splinters may be thrown by the cutting action of the knives.

- In-running nip points—Clothing, hair, or hands may be caught by and pulled into the in- running rolls of the automatic feed.

Engineering Controls

- As shown in Figure 17, enclose the spindle with an adjustable guard or cage [29 CFR 1910.213(m)(1)]. For straight-line shaping, the fence frame should include the guard. The fence should contain as small an opening as possible for the knives, and should extend at least 18 inches on either side of the spindle. Split adjustable fences are useful for guarding when the entire edge of the stock is to be shaped.

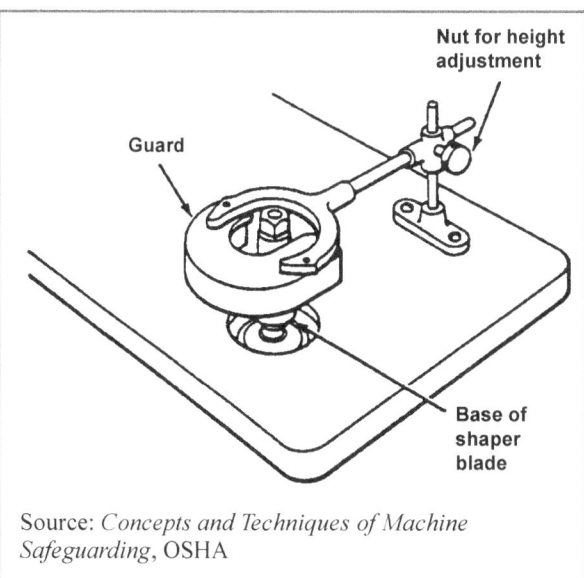

Nut for height adjustment

Guard

Base of shaper blade

Source: *Concepts and Techniques of Machine Safeguarding*, OSHA

Figure 17. Sharper with Adjustable Guard

- Mount a ring guard around the cutting bit to reduce contact with the bit.

- Guard automatic feed rollers [29 CFR 1910.213(b)(7)].

- Ensure that double-spindle shapers have a starting and stopping device for each spindle [29 CFR 1910.213(m)(3)].

- Use a safety collar to minimize the potential for tool projection.

Work Practices

- Maintain the knives. Make sure they are precision-ground to apply uniform pressure. Make sure the knives are balanced and fit properly [29 CFR 1910.213(s)(2)].

- Train operators to listen for "chatter," which indicates that knives are out of balance. To start the machine, operators should apply the power in a series of short starts and stops to slowly bring the spindle to operating speed.

- Use templates, jigs, and fixtures to distance the operator's hands from the point of operation. Featherboards may be clamped to the fence for straight line shaping.

- Cut in the opposite direction of the spindle's rotations.

Power-Feed Planers/Moulders

Also called surfacers, planers are used to dress and size rough-sawed lumber on one or more sides. They plane boards to an even thickness. Stock passes under or between cylindrical cutter heads with multiple knives. (See Figure 18.) Planers are similar to jointers except that the cutter head is above, or above and below, the stock. The operator adjusts for the cut and then feeds stock into the in-feed side of the machine. The surface board is retrieved from the out-running end.

Automatic feeding mechanisms make this equipment less hazardous. However, operators' hands may be pulled into the cutting area, and can come in contact with the point of operation while adjusting blades. Operators' hands also may be pinched between the stock and in-running rolls, if the feed system is not properly guarded.

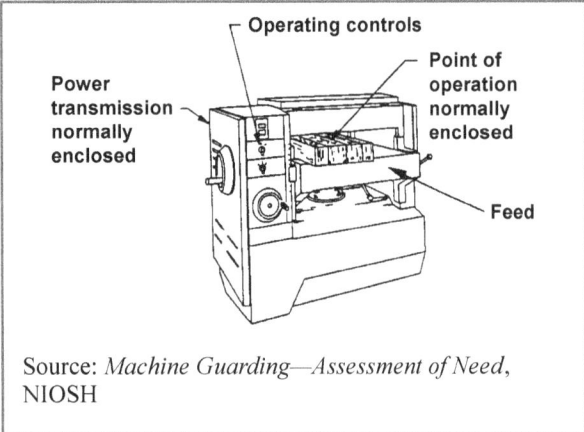

Source: *Machine Guarding—Assessment of Need*, NIOSH

Figure 18. Planer

Safety Hazards of Power-Feed Planers or Moulders

- Point of Operation—Contact with the cutter head may occur during blade adjustment or other maintenance activities.

- In-running rolls—Clothing, hair, or hands may be caught by and pulled into the automatic feed mechanism.

- Kickbacks—Stock may be thrown back at the operator after being caught by the cutter head.

- Flying objects—Workpiece, wood chips and splinters may be thrown by the cutting action.

- Vibration (and noise) may be produced if the machinery is not anchored to, and insulated from, a solid foundation

---

Engineering Controls

- Completely enclose belts and pulleys of line shaft with sheet metal or heavy mesh guards; guards must be used regardless of the location of the line shaft [29 CFR 1910.219(a)(1)].

- Cover cutting heads with a metal guard or cage. The exhaust system may be integrated with the guard [29 CFR 1910.213(n)(1)].

- Guard feed rolls with a wide metal strip or bar that will allow boards to pass but that will keep operators' fingers out [29 CFR 1910.213(n)(3)].

- Provide barriers at the loading and unloading ends to keep hands out of point of operation.

- Install anti-kickback fingers on the in-feed side across the width of the machine.

- Use a barrier or guardrail when the machine is running.

Work Practices

- Stand back once the boards have been put through to avoid injuries from kickback and flying splinters.

- Do not feed boards of different thicknesses. Thinner boards will be kicked back.

Lathes

Lathes are used for shaping round parts, such as table legs. Two types of lathes are used in the woodworking industry: automatic-feed and manual-feed. In an automatic-feed lathe, the stock, mounted on a carriage, is moved into contact with a multiple-knife cutter head that runs the entire length of the stock. The stock rotates at a low speed, while the cutter rotates faster. Using a feed lever, the operator feeds the stock into the cutter head and maintains the proper pressure for effective cutting.

In a hand-fed lathe, the stock, mounted between two centers, rotates rapidly while the operator applies a single-point tool to the wood. The operator holds the tool on a tool rest and advances it along the length of the tool rest to shape the stock as desired.

The primary hazards of lathes are contact with rotating parts and contact at the point of operation. Operators' hands, clothing, or jewelry may be caught on the rotating parts and pulled into the machine. The danger is greater with hand-fed lathes, because the operator works in such close proximity to the rotating stock and the cutting tool. With automatic lathes, the operator can contact the rotating parts if he or she reaches into the work area to adjust components while the machine is running. Flying chips are also a hazard on lathes.

Safety Hazards of Lathes

- Point of operation—Contact with the tool or cutter head may occur.

- Rotating parts—Clothing, hair, or hands may be caught by and pulled into the cutter or the rotating stock.

- Flying chips—Wood splinters and chips may be thrown by the cutting action.

- Kickback—The workpiece may be thrown out.

Engineering Controls

- For automatic wood-turning lathes with rotating knives, cover the cutter head with a metal shield or hood that completely covers the knives and material, except at the contact points, when the machine is in operation [29 CFR 1910.213(o)(3)]. A hinged shield permits adjustments when needed.

- For manual lathes, cover the cutter heads as completely as possible with a hood or shield [29 CFR 1910.213(o)(2)].

- Cover lathes used for turning long stock with long curved guards extending over the top of the lathe [29 CFR 1910.213(o)(4)]. Such guards prevent the stock from being thrown from the machine, should the stock come loose.

- Install a brake for bringing the stock to a complete stop after the power is shut off.

- On hand-fed lathes, guard the tool and point of operation with a plexiglass tool guard, as shown in Figure 19.

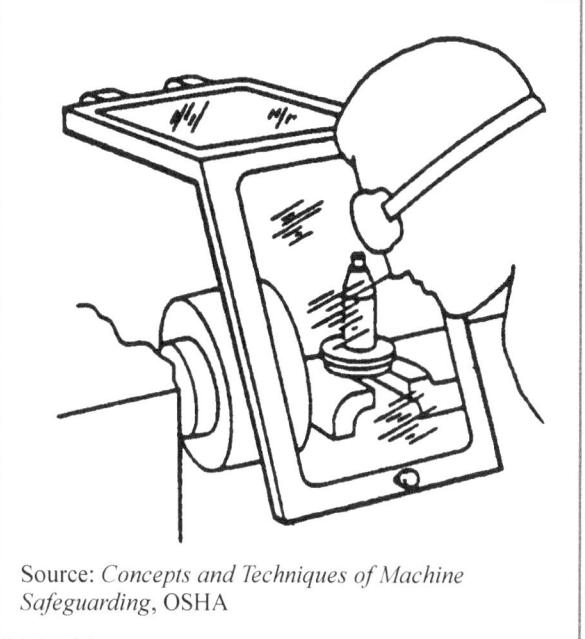

Source: *Concepts and Techniques of Machine Safeguarding*, OSHA

Figure 19. Plexiglass Guard on Lathe Protects Operator from Flying Chips

- Enclose the power transmission with a fixed guard [29 CFR 1910.219].

Work Practices

- Never permit operators to wear loose clothing, long hair, jewelry, or gloves.

- Make sure tools are properly adjusted and used in a proper manner.

- Do not use stock that has checks, splits, cracks, or knots.

- Allow glued joints to dry before working on stock.

- Hold tools firmly in both hands.

- Make sure the tool rest is set close to the stock. Work only in the area covered by the tool rest; do not attempt to support the tool with your hands. Adjust the tool rest when the lathe is not running.

Sanders

Sanders finish stock by using a coated abrasive surface to remove material. Figures 20 and 21 show the three general types of sanders: drum, belt, and disc. A belt sander uses a system of pulleys to move the abrasive material across the stock. Either the wood is fed manually or automatically into the machine or the sanding belt is pressed toward the wood, which is located on a working table.

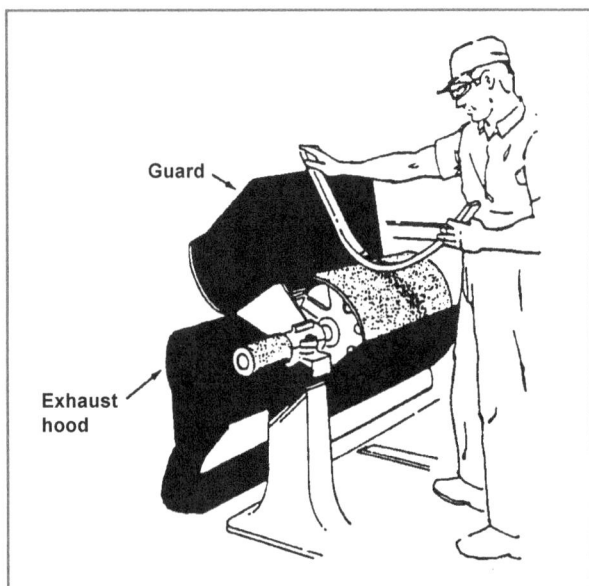

Figure 20. Drum Sander

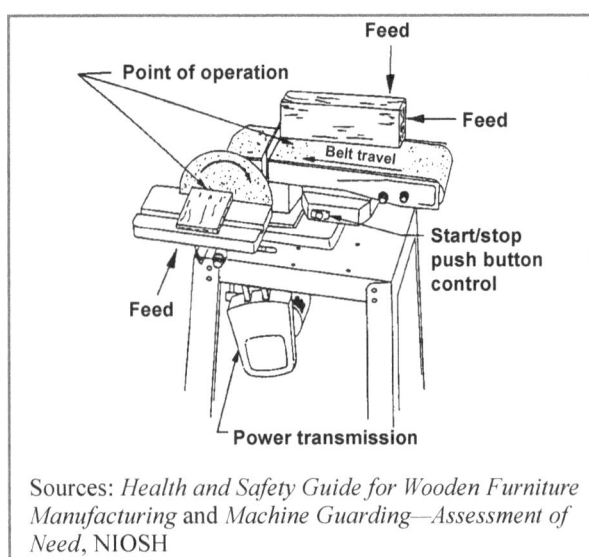

Sources: *Health and Safety Guide for Wooden Furniture Manufacturing* and *Machine Guarding—Assessment of Need*, NIOSH

Figure 21. Belt and Disc Sander

Sanders produce a considerable quantity of fine wood dust. Wood dust hazards and controls are discussed in detail in the section "How Can I Protect My Employees from Wood Dust?" All sanders should be carefully ventilated. The primary safety hazard of belt sanders is that workers may catch their hands, clothing, or jewelry in the in-running rolls. Also, contact with an abrasive surface can cause abrasions and lacerations.

Safety Hazards of Sanders

- Point of operation—Contact with disc or drum may occur.
- In-running nip points—Clothing, hands, or hair may get caught by and pulled into the in-running rolls on automatic sanders or sanding belts.
- Flying chips—Wood splinters and chips may be thrown from the sanding action.

Engineering Controls

- Guard feed rolls with a semi-cylindrical guard to prevent the operator's hands from coming in contact with the in-running rolls on automatic sanders. The guard design must allow for adjustment to any thickness of stock [29 CFR 1910.213(p)(1)].
- Guard the unused run of the sanding belt against accidental contact. These guards must prevent the operator's hands or fingers from coming in contact with nip points [29 CFR 1910.219].
- Enclose drum and disc sanders with guards, except for the portion of the sander's drum above the table. The guard can consist of a protective cover at the rear side of the wheel and a hinged cover around the wheel periphery [29 CFR 1910.213(p)(2) and (p)(3)].
- Enclose power transmission pulleys with a fixed guard [29 CFR 1910.219].

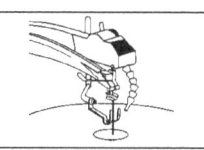
Work Practices

- Replace torn, frayed, or excessively worn belts or drums. A worn-out belt, disk, or drum can cause massive heat buildup, which can cause the belt, disk, or drum to tear or break and pelt the surrounding area with projected bits.
- Keep hands away from abrasive surfaces.
- Sand on the downward-moving side of the disk or belt.

Routers

Routers are used for such purposes as cutting and shaping decorative pieces, making frame and panel doors, and milling moldings. Routers have spindles that spin variously shaped, small-diameter cutting tools at high speeds. The tool is held in a collet chuck and protrudes through a flat, smooth base that slides over the surface of the work. The tool-spindle axis is usually vertical, but it may be tilted. The operator lowers the head for machining, and the head automatically returns to its original position after the cut is made. The spindle is driven by belts and pulleys or by a high-speed motor.

Operators may be injured from inadvertent contact with the rotating tool when handling the stock or removing scrap from the table. Kickback is another common source of injury among router operators. Kickback may be caused by poor-quality lumber (i.e., if the stock breaks) or incorrect work method, such as feeding the stock into the tool too abruptly or in the wrong direction, or poorly fixing the stock to the template.

Projection of tools can severely injure or kill router operators. Tools can be flung from the cutter head if they are poorly fastened in the tool holder, if the wrong tool is used, or if the tool speed is too high.

Safety Hazards of Routers

- Point of operation—Contact with the cutter head may occur.
- Rotating parts—Clothing or hair may be caught on rotating cutter head.
- Tool projection—Knives may be thrown from unbalanced or improperly adjusted cutter heads, or from cutter heads operated with tools that were not designed for the cutter head.
- Flying chips—Wood chips or wood dust, and splinters may be thrown by the cutting action.

Engineering Controls

- Enclose the tool with an adjustable tool guard, as shown in Figure 22 [29 CFR 1910.213(m)(1)].

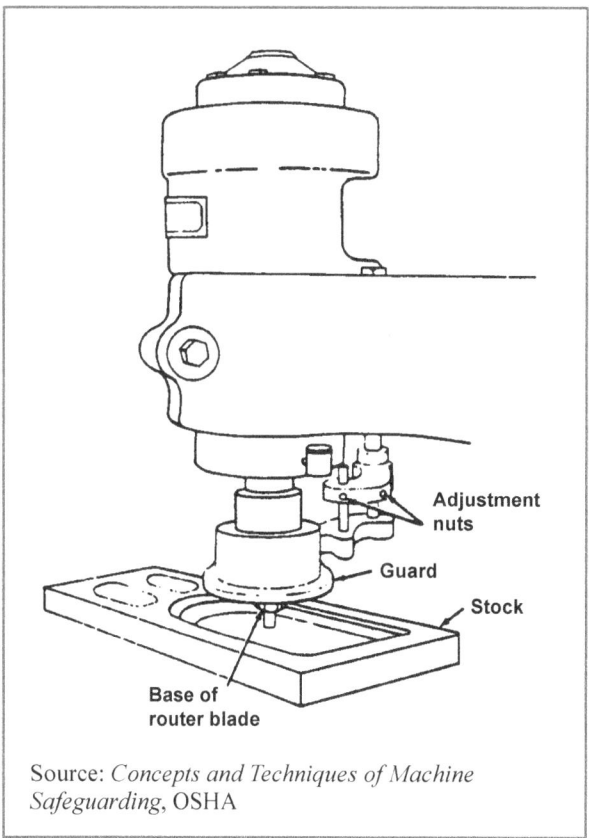

Source: *Concepts and Techniques of Machine Safeguarding*, OSHA

Figure 22. Router with Adjustable Tool Guard

• Equip routers with a spindle braking system that gradually engages.

• Guard feed rolls [29 CFR 1910.213(b)(7)].

Work Practices

• Properly attach and secure tools to the holder.

• Label cutting tools and holders with the maximum permissible spindle speed.

• Use tools only as intended.

Tenoning Machine

Tenoning machines use cutter heads and/or saw blades to form projections (tenons) on pieces of stock. Each tenon can be inserted into a cavity (mortise) on another piece of wood to form a mortise and tenon joint. Figure 23 shows a single-end tenoning machine.

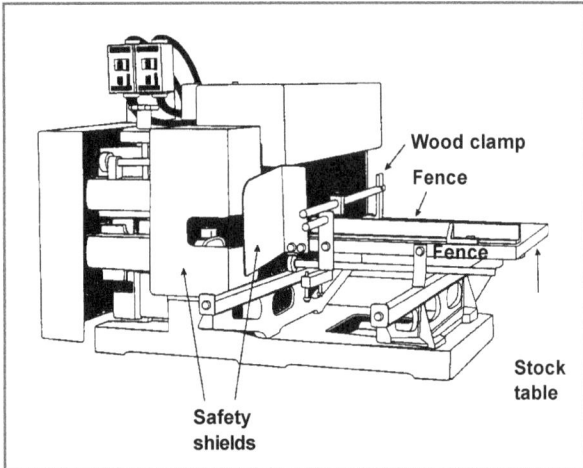

Figure 23. Single-End Tenoning Machine

Safety Hazards of Tenoning Machines

• Point of operation—Contact with cutter head or saw blade may occur.

• In-running nip points—Clothing, hair, or hands may be caught by and pulled into the in-running rolls of the automatic feed.

• Flying chips—Wood splinters and chips may be thrown by the cutting action.

• Kickbacks—Stock may be thrown back at the operator after being caught by the cutter head or saw blade.

Engineering Controls

• Enclose feed chains and sprockets of double end machines, except for the portion of the chain conveying stock [29 CFR 1910.213(k)(1)].

• The cutting head and saws must be guarded with metal guards. Cover the unused part of the periphery of the cutting head. If an exhaust system is used, the guard must form part of the exhaust system [29 CFR 1910.213(k)(3)].

Boring/Mortising Machine

Boring and mortising machines use boring bits or mortising chains to cut cavities in pieces of stock. These cavities are often used in mortise and tenon joints. Figure 24 shows a chain mortising machine.

Safety Hazards of Boring/Mortising Machines

• Point of operation—Contact with the boring bit or mortising chain may occur.

• Rotating parts—Clothing or hair may be caught on rotating boring bit or mortising chain.

• In-running nip points—Clothing, hair, or hands may be caught by and pulled into in- running rolls of automatic feed.

• Flying chips—Woods chips and splinters may be thrown by the cutting action.

• Kickbacks—Stock may be thrown back at operator.

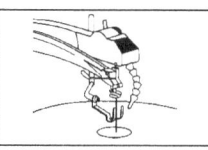
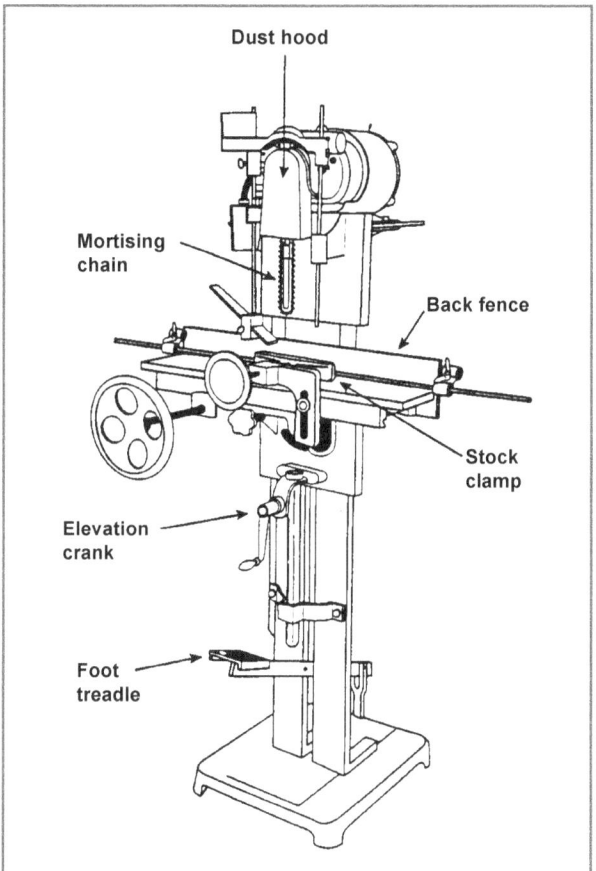

Dust hood

Mortising chain

Back fence

Stock clamp

Elevation crank

Foot treadle

Figure 24. Chain Mortising Machine

Engineering Controls

- Use safety bit chucks with no projecting screws [29 CFR 1910.213(l)(1)].

- Enclose boring bits with a guard that encloses the bit and chuck above the material being worked [29 CFR 1910.213(l)(2)].

- Enclose the top of the cutting chain and driving mechanism [29 CFR 1910.213(l)(3)].

- If a counterweight is used, prevent it from dropping by bolting it to the bar or attaching a safety chain to it [29 CFR 1910.213(l)(4)].

- Cover operating treadles with inverted U-shaped guard to prevent accidental tripping [29 CFR 1910.213(l)(6)].

What Are Other Safety Hazards of Woodworking?

Other safety hazards associated with woodworking equipment include electrical hazards, fire and explosion hazards, and hazards caused by poor machine maintenance.

What Are the Electrical Hazards?

Electrical hazards include electrocution, fire, or explosions. Even slight shocks can lead to injury or death.

How Can I Protect My Employees from Electrical Hazards?

All electrical installations must comply with OSHA electrical standards. Among the many provisions included in the standards are the following requirements:

- All of the metal framework on electrically driven machines must be grounded, including the motor, motor casing, legs, and frame. This includes other equipment such as lights that may be mounted on the machine.
- All circuit breakers and fuse boxes must be labeled to indicate their purpose—that is, what area of the plant they power or protect. Appropriately rated fuses must be used. All unused holes in electric boxes must be covered.
- Electrical cords, cables, and plugs must be kept in good repair. Flexible cords and cables must be fastened so that there is no direct pull on joints or terminal screws. Cords and cables must be free of splices and must not run through windows, doorways, or holes in the wall.
- Junction boxes, outlets, switches, and fittings must be covered.
- All electrical components must be approved by a Nationally Recognized Testing Laboratory for the specific location where the equipment will be used.
- All machines must have a main power disconnect for lockout/tagout.

In addition, all machines should have the following:

- A magnetic switch or other device to prevent automatic restarting of the machine after a power failure. Such an unexpected start-up could expose the worker to moving parts.
- An emergency stop device (panic bar or deadman switch) within reach of operators working in the normal operating position.
- Clearly marked controls that are within easy reach of the operator and away from the hazard area.

What Are the Machine Maintenance Hazards?

Each year, more than a hundred workers are killed, and many more are injured, while repairing or maintaining machines.[2] A coworker may start a machine that another employee is repairing. Sometimes it is the worker who accidentally knocks a switch and energizes the machine while clearing a jam or cleaning the equipment. Workers may be crushed at the point of operation, drawn into rotating parts, instantly electrocuted, or mangled by other moving parts. To prevent accidental energizing of machines during maintenance, shut off and lock out all power sources. Under OSHA's Lockout/Tagout standard, 29 CFR 1910.147, tagout is permitted if an energy-isolating device is not capable of being locked out or if certain other conditions apply.

How Can I Protect My Employees from Machine Maintenance Hazards?

You can protect your workers by establishing a "lockout/tagout" program. Lockout/tagout refers to the process of shutting down and locking out machines before maintenance begins to prevent accidental start-up during machine maintenance, cleaning, or other similar operations. Locking out equipment provides a physical means (i.e., a lock) that ensures that power will not be restored to the machine and that the machine will not be started until work on the machine has been completed. Tagging the equipment warns others that someone is working on the machine and that power must not

_____

[2] From Bureau of Labor Statistics. 1995. *Fatal Workplace Injuries in 1993: A Collection of Data and Analysis.* U.S. Department of Labor, p.78.

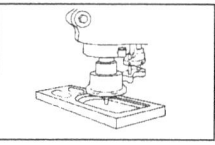
be restored to the machine until the work is completed and the person performing the work removes the tag.

All power sources—electrical, mechanical, pneumatic, hydraulic—must be shut off and locked out during machine maintenance. This includes power that is stored in a machine, such as compressed air in a cylinder, after the machine is turned off. To achieve this, you must have a written lockout/tagout plan that, for each machine, describes all power sources and the correct procedure for shutting down, testing, and re-energizing the equipment. Your plan should describe how employees will be notified when a lockout/tagout is necessary, and shall require your employees to always lock out or tag out equipment, using the appropriate procedures, before performing work on the equipment.

How Can I Develop an Effective Lockout and Tagout Program?

To develop your energy control program, inventory your equipment and identify all power sources. Identify the lockout devices that you will need for your particular machines. There are many commercially available devices for locking out electrical switches, circuit breakers, valves, compressed-air lines, hydraulic equipment, and other power sources. When feasible, affected employees must be given their own lock to use during lockout procedures. If you use tagout devices in place of lockout devices, the tagout program must be as effective as the lockout program. Train all affected employees about your company's plan: your program will only work if your employees understand how to implement the correct lockout/tagout procedures. See the "Resources" section of this guide for more information on lockout/tagout controls. OSHA's standard, 29 CFR 1910.147, establishes specific requirements for lockout/tagout programs. Refer to this standard for more information on how to properly protect your workers.

Is My Facility Susceptible to Fire and Explosion?

Yes. Woodworking facilities are inherently prone to fires and explosions, for the following reasons:

- They contain large quantities of fuel in the form of wood and wood products, sawdust, and flammable materials such as paints, oil finishes, adhesives, solvents, and liquid propane for internal combustion engines. Woodworking facilities are especially at risk for fire due to the abundant production of sawdust, which will ignite and burn far more easily than whole pieces of lumber. Sanders, routers, and shapers in particular produce large amounts of fine dust. Very fine wood dust is especially hazardous. It can accumulate on rafters and other building structural components and in unexpected spots all around your facility, far from the point of generation.

- They contain ignition sources, such as potentially faulty electrical wiring, cutting and welding operations, sparking tools, propellant-actuated tools, and employee smoking. There is also the potential for static electrical discharges and lightning.

Conduct at least an annual inspection of the lockout/tagout program to ensure that it is followed.

How Can I Protect My Employees and Facility from Fires and Explosions ?

Preventing the buildup of dust is one of the key means for controlling fire and explosion hazards. The principal engineering control technology for control of dust is exhaust ventilation. The primary work practice control is good housekeeping.

Dust collection is best accomplished at the source—at the point of operation of the equipment, if feasible. For many pieces of equipment, well-designed ducts and vacuum hoods can collect most of the dust generated before it even reaches the operator. Very fine dust that manages to escape point-of-source collection can be captured from above by general exhaust points located along the ceiling. These control technologies are effective for most equipment, excepting machines that commonly produce the very finest dust or large quantities of dust.

Good housekeeping extends to periodic hand cleaning of your entire facility, as some dust will escape from even the best exhaust system and will eventually accumulate on rafters and other out-of-the-way spots. Also, it is extremely important to inspect and clean your exhaust ventilation system on a regular basis to maintain maximum efficiency.

You must also:

- Ensure the proper use and storage of flammable materials, such as paints, finishes, adhesives, and solvents.
- Segregate tasks particularly prone to fire and explosion hazards, such as spray painting, welding, and use of powder-actuated nail guns.
- Train employees to recognize, avoid, and correct potentially hazardous conditions and behaviors. Train employees so that they are acquainted with the special equipment and aspects of building design related to dealing with fires and explosions.
- Control ignition sources. This involves using electrical systems rated for the projected use and protected by appropriate circuit breakers, grounding all equipment prone to accumulating static electrical charges, grounding entire buildings against the possibility of lightning strikes, and controlling and banning smoking in and around the workplace. Consult Subpart S of OSHA's General Industry Standards for more information on electrical design requirements.
- Never permit blow-down of accumulated dust with compressed air. Blowing dust with compressed air will create the very type of dust cloud that presents the greatest explosion hazard.
- Provide continuous local exhaust ventilation on all woodworking machines. The local exhaust systems must have a suitable collector. Dust collection systems must be located outside the building, unless the exceptions described in NFPA standards are met.
- Segregate combustible and flammable materials such as lumber stock and chemical solvents from each other and from ignition sources.
- Ensure that you use equipment with a hazard classification appropriately rated for your work environment.

What Other Fire Protection Measures Should Be Taken?

- Fire-resistant construction and/or fire-resistant materials (particularly fire doors that could be used to contain the spread of a fire).
- Explosion relief devices, such as blow-out panels in walls, floors, and ceilings that protect structural integrity in the event of an explosion.
- Multiple emergency exits that are well marked and easily accessible. These exits should lead people directly away from the areas of greatest likely hazard.
- Emergency alarms and communications systems to promote rapid evacuation and fire fighting response.
- Automatic sprinkler systems designed for a worst-case fire scenario.
- Readily accessible, portable fire extinguishers fully charged with fire retardants appropriate to the types of fires likely to occur in that area.

What Should You Do to Protect Your Workers in the Event of a Fire?

- Install an alarm system to warn for necessary action or safe escape [29 CFR 1910.165].
- Establish emergency plans and fire prevention plans [29 CFR 1910.38].
- Install battery-operated emergency lighting along the floor to aid in the evacuation of smoke- filled buildings.
- Store fire-retardant blankets, clothing, and masks in areas where workers could conceivably need them to pass through smoke and flames to reach exits.
- Maintain first-aid kits designed for the initial treatment of burns and smoke inhalation. These kits should be stored outside the area of fire risk.

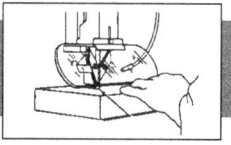
What Are the Health Hazards of Wood Dust?

Exposure to wood dust has long been associated with a variety of adverse health effects, including dermatitis, allergic respiratory effects, mucosal and nonallergic respiratory effects, and cancer. Contact with the irritant compounds in wood sap can cause dermatitis and other allergic reactions. The respiratory effects of wood dust exposure include asthma, hypersensitivity pneumonitis, and chronic bronchitis.

Both the skin and respiratory system can become sensitized to wood dust. When a worker becomes sensitized to wood dust, he or she can suffer a severe allergic reaction (such as asthma) after repeated exposure or exposure to lower concentrations of the dust.

Other common symptoms associated with wood dust exposure include eye irritation, nasal dryness and obstruction, prolonged colds, and frequent headaches.

Certain species of hardwood—such as oak, mahogany, beech, walnut, birch, elm, and ash— have been reported to cause nasal cancer in woodworkers. This is particularly true when exposures are high. The American Conference of Governmental Industrial Hygienists (ACGIH) recognizes wood dust as a "confirmed" human carcinogen,[3] and recommends a limit of 1 milligram per cubic meter (mg/m^3) for hardwoods and 5 mg/m^3 for softwoods. At this time, OSHA regulates wood dust as a nuisance dust; however, OSHA strongly encourages employers to keep exposures to a minimum and to adopt the ACGIH levels. The maximum permissible exposure for nuisance dust is 15 mg/m^3, total dust (5 mg/m^3, respirable fraction).

How Can I Protect My Employees from Wood Dust?

Employers can protect workers from wood dust through a combination of engineering and work

---

[3] *ACGIH Threshold Limit Values for Chemical Substances and Physical Agents—Biological Exposure Indices, 1996.*

practice controls. Where necessary, employers must provide PPE as a supplement to these controls.

Engineering Controls

Wood dust is emitted at high velocity by moving or spinning machine components. The primary method of controlling wood dust is with local exhaust ventilation (LEV), which removes dust at or near its source. LEV systems can often be integrated with machine guards. Exhaust hoods should be located as close as possible to the emission source, either on the woodworking machinery itself or near to the machine. The local exhaust systems should have an efficient air cleaning device.

How Can I Maintain Local Exhaust Ventilation?

For LEV systems to provide maximum protection, they should be properly maintained. Check and clean ducts and dust collectors at regular intervals. Inspect ducts to ensure that they are not loose, broken, or damaged. Check the V-belts on the drive units of belt-driven exhaust fans for slippage or breakage. Make sure the duct velocity is maintained at a minimum of 2,500 to 4,000 feet per minute to effectively remove light, dry saw dust, heavy wood chips, and green shavings, and to prevent these from plugging the system.

Sanders, shapers, and routers generally produce the greatest amount of dust. Conventional means for exhausting these machines are not very effective. NIOSH has developed new, innovative means for controlling dust exposure from these machines, but these methods are not yet commercially available. These methods either increase the exhaust volume or velocity, or supply pressurized air to help blow dust particles from the machine into an exhaust hood.

Work Practices

See the discussion for control of fire and explosion hazards ("How Can I Protect My Employees and Facility from Fire and Explosion Hazards") for information on work practices to control dust accumulations.

LEV Recommendations for Individual Machines

Circular Saws

- Exhaust the saw through the bottom of the table. Provide LEV under the blade slot. To decrease the open area between the table and the lower hood, attach a strip of flexible material to the machinery that will cover this area when the hood operates.

- For increased dust control, add a local exhaust hood above the top of the saw blade. The hood should be integrated with the guard on the upper part of the blade.

- For further information on control of wood dust from circular and other kinds of table saws, please consult the NIOSH Hazard Controls HC10 (See Appendix B).

Band Saws

- Provide LEV under the blade slot. To increase the collection area of the hood, add holes (1/8 inch in diameter) in the table around the slot area.

- To collect wood dust from the saw teeth, place a suction nozzle above the table, at the rear of the saw blade.

Jointers

- Place a hood underneath the machine head.

Shapers

- Control each head with an open-faced hood, located on the table behind the head. For additional protection, use a combination of fixed and adjustable hoods. A fixed open-faced hood can be attached to the rear of the table between the shaper heads. Movable open-faced hoods also can be used on the table. For further information please consult the NIOSH Hazard Controls HC5: Wood Dust from Shapers (See Appendix B).

Planers/Moulders

- Place open-faced hoods above the spinning heads of planers. Each head can be ventilated separately, or one hood can be used to control several heads.

- Place open-faced hoods around the spinning components of moulders. Each head should be separately controlled.

- For increased dust control, add a small open-faced hood along the side of the moulder between the main head and the worker.

Lathes

- Place an open-faced hood attached to a movable mechanical arm at the point of operation.

Sanders

Sanders produce a considerable amount of dust and are difficult to control. Conventional methods do not effectively remove dust. New innovative systems have been developed for controlling dust emissions from horizontal belt sanders, large-diameter disc sanders, random orbital hand sanders, and orbital hand sanders. Although these systems are not yet commercially available, more information can be obtained from the National Institute for Occupational Safety and Health (NIOSH). The following NIOSH Hazard Controls deal with horizontal belt sanders, large diameter disc sanders, random orbital hand sanders and orbital hand sanders respectively: HC4, HC 7, HC 8 and HC 9 (See Appendix B). Some of these systems are discussed below.

- Enclose disc sanders with an exhaust hood, installed below the table; cover the back of the sanding disc at points above the worktable. A system has been developed that supplies pressurized air to the disc inside the hood. The jet of high speed air blows dust particles out of the disc air layer so that they can be captured by the exhaust hood.

- On random orbital sanders, use an aspirator in combination with a perforated sanding pad. The aspirator creates a vacuum that draws wood dust up through the holes of the sanding pad. An innovative dust control system has been developed that uses additional exhaust and a slotted sanding pad.

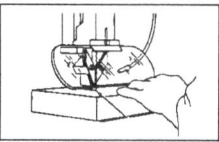
Other Sources of Information on Wood Dust Control

NIOSH has published a series of "Hazard Controls" concerning wood dust control techniques. For details see Appendix B.

- A new dust control plenum has been designed for orbital sanders. The plenum fits between the sanding pad and the sander body and has a series of exhaust slots along its edges.

- Enclose horizontal belt sanders with exhaust hoods covering each end of the belt. These hoods control the dust carried by the belt. To further control dust emissions, install an additional hood above the area where the wood is processed. To increase the effectiveness of this system, add a narrow hood and a stripper.

Routers
- Place two open-faced hoods behind the heads of the router table. Connect the hoods to the exhaust ductwork via a flexible hose.

- Locate an open-faced or slot hood at the rear end of the router table.

- For further information please consult the NIOSH Hazard Controls HC6: Wood Dust from Automated Routers (See Appendix B).

What Are the Health Hazards of Noise?

Excessive noise can damage a person's ability to hear—an effect that can be temporary or permanent. There also is mounting evidence that noise may adversely affect other parts of the body—particularly the cardiovascular, endocrine, and muscular systems—and may also lead to stress-related disorders, such as nervousness, chronic fatigue, increased blood pressure, and impaired concentration and mental function. There are as yet no effective treatments for noise-induced health problems, beyond the body's limited natural ability to repair itself, over time, with rest and quiet.

What Constitutes Dangerous Noise and Is It a Problem at My Business?

Two primary factors act together to make noise hazardous—volume (intensity) and duration. The louder the noise and the longer the duration of exposure at that volume, the greater the potential for hearing loss. The risk of hearing impairment is also cumulative over the course of a working day.

The frequency of a sound is measured in units called hertz—one hertz equaling one vibration cycle per second. The normal range of human hearing encompasses sounds with frequencies from 20 to 20,000 hertz. Sound pressure is commonly measured on the A-weighted decibel (dBA) scale, where zero decibels is the weakest sound that can be heard by a person with very good hearing in an extremely quiet location.

Table 4 shows the accepted daily exposure limits to various noise levels. For example, a circular saw operator exposed to 105 dBA reaches the threshold for hearing damage in 1 hour, while a worker operating a vacuum at 95 dBA can safely work for 4 hours. Another worker could run the circular saw for half an hour and then vacuum 2 hours before reaching the limit for noise exposure. However, none of these workers could be exposed to occupational noise in excess of 90 dBA for the rest of the day.

Decibel levels from two or more sounds cannot be simply added. The combined effect of two sounds depends on the difference in their levels. When there is no difference in the sound levels between two sources, the combined effect will be an increase of 3 dBA. For example, if two circular saws are placed side by side, and each has a noise level of 105 dBA, the resulting noise level from both machines would be 108 dBA. Once the difference in noise level between two sources reaches 10 dBA or more, however, the combined sound level is essentially that of the louder source. Thus, if someone is vacuuming next to a circular saw operator, both workers will only hear the saw.

What Are My Options for Noise Control?

You can reduce noise levels through the use of some or all of the simple and practical methods discussed below. These methods focus on three basic approaches to controlling noise: noise source controls, noise path controls, and hearing protection. Noise source controls, which typically consist of engineering controls, provide the most effective means of protection, since they actually reduce the amount of noise generated in the workplace. For this reason, it is best to exhaust source control options first, before moving on to path controls and, finally, to hearing protection devices.

Source Controls

Source control begins with a thorough analysis of each piece of noise-generating equipment. You should attempt to identify all noise sources within a given piece of equipment, as well as the ways in which the sound is transmitted (and often amplified via resonance or vibration) to the surrounding room. Then every effort should be made to both quiet the sources and dampen the resonant pathways of transmission. Noise sources generally include motors, gears, belts and pulleys, points of operation where blades touch wood, and any other moving parts. Resonant transmitters generally include the frames, footings, and housings of the equipment.

Examples of source control steps include the following:

- Maintaining motors and all moving parts in top operating condition. Maintenance involves lubricating and cleaning; replacing worn parts; maintaining proper belt tensions and bolt torques; and properly balancing pulleys, blades, and other rotating parts.

- Reducing the speed of operation of the equipment to the slowest level consistent with product quantity and quality goals.

- Moving power equipment operations out of wooden or steel-frame buildings and into stone, cement, or brick structures, if at all possible.

- Ensuring that equipment frames are as rigid as possible, that equipment is firmly seated on a solid floor (preferably cement slab), and that no piece of equipment is in contact with any other piece or with walls.

- Isolating noisy equipment with rubber footings, springs, or other forms of damping suspension so as to reduce the radiation and amplification of noise via vibrations.

- Applying vibration-damping materials to all resonating surfaces, and constructing (where possible) sound absorbent hoods around points of operation.

Table 4. Allowable Daily Noise Exposure Limits—Unprotected

Exposure Duration (hours)	Noise Level (dBA)	Representative Source
8	90	electric ventilation fan
6	92	drill press
4	95	shop vacuum
3	97	drum sander
2	100	emergency siren
1.5	102	wood planer
1	105	circular saw
0.5	110	chain saw
0.25	115	jackhammer
No tolerance	140	power-driven nail gun

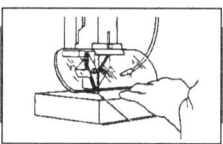

Path Controls

Effective path controls involve isolating, blocking, diverting, absorbing, or otherwise reducing noise intensity before it reaches your employees' ears.

Examples of path control steps include

• Segregating operations so as to limit, as far as possible, the number of employees exposed to excessive equipment noise.

• Enclosing equipment within barriers designed to absorb noise and/or reflect it in harmless directions, such as toward ceilings covered with sound absorbent material.

• Moving or locating noise-producing equipment away from employees, since noise intensity decreases significantly as you move away from the source of the noise. Depending on the types of surfaces in your workplace, you can reduce the level of noise that your workers are exposed to by up to 6 dBA by doubling the distance between the source of the noise and your workers. The presence of reflective surfaces (such as flat metal surfaces) in the workplace will reduce the level of noise reduction achieved by this method.

Hearing Protection

Hearing protection devices isolate the human ear from harmful noises. They should be worn by your employees as the final line of defense against noise hazards. Hearing protection devices can be effective and, compared to source and path control efforts, relatively inexpensive. Their use, however, does demand a considerable level of ongoing effort and commitment.

Given the nature of woodworking operations, your production floor employees will almost certainly require hearing protection devices. Please refer to the "Personal Protective Equipment" section of this guide for more information about hearing protection devices and about selecting appropriate devices for your employees.

What Are the Health Hazards of Vibration?

Both hand-held and stationary tools that transmit vibration through a work piece can cause vibration "white fingers" or hand-arm vibration syndrome (HAVS). White fingers, or Raynaud's Syndrome, is a disease of the hands in which the blood vessels in the fingers collapse due to repeated exposure to vibration. The skin and muscle tissue do not get the oxygen they need and eventually die. HAVS is a more advanced condition, and the entire hand or arm may be affected by exposure to vibration. Early signs of HAVS are infrequent feelings of numbness and/or tingling in the fingers, hands, or arms, or numbness and whiteness in the tip of the finger when exposed to cold. As the disease progresses, a worker experiences more frequent attacks of numbness, tingling, and pain and finds it difficult to use his or her hands. A worker with advanced HAVS may be disabled for a long time.

How Can I Protect My Workers from Vibration?

Engineering Controls

Vibration isolators or damping techniques on equipment offer the most effective protection. Isolate machine vibrations from the surface if it is mounted or by use of vibration isolation mounts. Vibrating panels of machine housings and guards may be controlled by use of damping materials applied to the panels. Felts, liquid mastics, and elastomeric damping sheets are effective damping materials. Determining the correct type and quantity of damping material to use for a particular machine is a complicated process and should be left to a knowledgeable person. The frequency emitted by the machine, the noise reduction level desired, and the weight and size of the machine are factors to consider. A good rule of thumb, however, is that the damping layer should be the same thickness as the surfaces being treated.

Work Practices

- Maintain machines in proper working order. Unbalanced rotating parts or unsharpened cutting tools can give off excessive vibration.

- Arrange work tasks so that vibrating and nonvibrating tools can be used alternately.

- Restrict the number of hours a worker uses a vibrating tool during the workday. Allow employees to take 10 to 15 minute breaks from the source of the vibration every hour.

- Train workers about the hazards of working with vibrating tools. Instruction should include: the sources of vibration exposure, early signs and symptoms of hand-arm vibration syndrome, and work practices for minimizing vibration exposure.

- Instruct workers to keep their hands warm and dry, and to not grip a vibrating tool too tightly. Workers should allow the tool or machine to do the work.

The preceding sections of this guide discuss ways of recognizing and controlling health and safety hazards at your facility. Once you have implemented all relevant engineering and work-practice controls, ask yourself (and your employees) what potential hazards remain. If hazards continue to exist, you must provide your employees with the necessary personal protective equipment (PPE) to supplement engineering and work practice controls and thoroughly protect your employees.

What Is PPE?

The term "personal protective equipment" refers to any device or garment worn by a worker on the job to safeguard against injuries and/or the harmful effects of hazardous substances. A wide variety of effective PPE can be readily obtained to protect workers' eyes, hearing, respiratory tracts, and body parts (for example, head, feet, hands, and arms). Table 5 lists some of the PPE items typically required in woodworking facilities.

Table 5. PPE Items Typically Used in the Woodworking Industry

* Hard hats
* Safety glasses, goggles, and face shields
* Gloves (including chemically protective gloves)
* Padded kickback aprons; vests; and arm, groin, and leg guards
* Lower-back supports
* Steel-shanked, steel-toed safety shoes with slip-resistant soles
* Earplugs and earmuffs
* Particulate-resistant and/or chemically resistant overalls
* Respirators

The remaining hazards in your facility may include:

* Blows to the head from stock and equipment at certain locations within your manufacturing and shipping operations.
* Threats to the eyes and face from flying wood chips and splinters, dust, and machine parts.
* Cutting and tearing hazards, particularly to the hands and arms, during equipment operations.
* The threat of kickback blows to the body, groin, and legs during stock-cutting and shaping.
* Crushing and laceration threats to the feet, particularly around loading equipment (for example, forklifts) and hand-held power tools (such as chain saws).
* Irritation of the skin, mouth, nose, throat, and lungs from dust, paint, adhesives, and other chemicals.
* The constant threat to hearing from machine noise.

PPE designed to protect against such hazards may range from hard hats and earplugs to chemically resistant overalls and respirators. A description of how PPE can protect against these woodworking hazards is provided below. For a more detailed discussion on the proper selection and use of PPE, refer to OSHA's pamphlet *Assessing the Need for Personal Protective Equipment (PPE): A Guide for Small Business Employers* (OSHA 3151). (See Appendix A for more information.)

Eye Protection

Where appropriate, you must provide eye protection to guard against flying particles (for example, wood chips and dust), as well as the risk of paint splashes and other chemical hazards. OSHA requires that all protective eyewear used in the woodworking industry meet the specifications of the American National Standards Institute (ANSI Z87.1-1989).[4] The eye protection that you choose must meet the criteria listed in Table 6.

---

[4] *ANSI, 11 West 42nd St., New York, NY 10035*

Table 6. Minimum Criteria for Selecting ANSI-Approved Eye Protection

- Provides adequate protection against the hazards of your workplace.
- Is reasonably comfortable for your employees to wear.
- Does not restrict your employees' field or acuity of vision, nor their freedom of movement, except as necessary to provide protection.
- Is durable, and easy to clean and disinfect.
- Does not interfere with the function of other required PPE, such as respirators.

Employees responsible for different tasks at your facility may require (or prefer) different types of eye protection, including impact-resistant glasses with side shields, goggles, and full-face shields. These items each provide a specific kind of protection: safety glasses provide protection from impact eye injuries; goggles with limited venting provide protection from impact eye injuries, dust, and chemical splashes; and full-face shields extend dust and splash protection to the neck (although they should be used in combination with safety glasses or goggles to protect against significant impact hazards).

Employees who wear corrective lenses will require eye protection that provides vision correction. (Regular eyeglasses that do not meet the ANSI Z87.1 standards do not provide adequate protection.) For these employees you should provide one of the following:

- Prescription safety glasses,
- Goggles that fit well over their regular eyeglasses, or
- Goggles that incorporate corrective lenses mounted behind the protective lens.

Head Protection

You must provide protective helmets—hard hats—to employees exposed to overhead hazards. Such hazards occur in areas where:

- Equipment and/or materials are stored, operated, or in any way manipulated above shoulder level.
- Fixed objects, such as exposed pipes and beams, present low clearance.

Hard hats protect employees from objects that could fall on and/or strike their heads. Hard hats used in the woodworking industry must comply with the ANSI Z89.1-1986 standard. OSHA recommends Class A hard hats, which are designed for mining, construction, and manufacturing uses.

Foot and Leg Protection

You must provide foot and leg protection to your employees if they are subject to hazards such as:

- Heavy objects (for example, tools, equipment, fork lifts, heavy-duty dollies, drums, wood stock) rolling over, falling onto, or striking them in the feet or legs.
- Sharp objects (for example, broken saw teeth, broken router blades, nails, spikes, or other fasteners) piercing the soles or uppers of their shoes.
- Slippery surfaces.

The type of foot and leg protection you purchase for your employees should depend on the specific hazards in your facility, but the safety shoes must at least meet the ANSI Z41-1991 standards. Standard safety shoes or boots with slip-resistant soles, puncture-resistant shanks, and compression-resistant toes should suffice for your workers who require protection.

Your need for leg protection will probably be minimal and can be met, where necessary, with hard plastic shin/lower-leg guards for impact

resistance, and knee pads/guards where kneeling on hard surfaces is a regular part of the task performed.

Hand and Arm Protection

Your workers' hands and arms will need protection from burns, bruises, abrasions, cuts, and exposure to the chemicals used in finishing.

Protective gloves are the primary means available for direct hand protection. Extra-long gauntlets or sleeves attached to the gloves can extend protection up the arm. However, the appropriateness of glove use in the woodworking workplace should be carefully reviewed on a task-by-task basis. Gloves should not be worn when operating woodworking equipment due to the potential for getting caught in moving parts.

Heavy leather, metal mesh, or gloves may provide protection against cuts, abrasions, and lacerations, but they can also greatly reduce dexterity, possibly leading to a higher frequency of the mishaps they are intended to protect against. Furthermore, no glove will stand up to direct contact with the cutting surfaces of most of your power equipment. For these reasons, engineering and work-practice controls will be your best bet for addressing the hand and arm hazards posed by cutting and shaping equipment.

When it comes to handling wood finishes, adhesives, equipment cleansing solvents, or any other chemical compounds, you should provide appropriate gloves and make their use mandatory. Chemically resistant gloves are designed as impermeable barriers to prevent absorption of hazardous compounds through the skin of the hands. The most common gloves designed for this purpose are composed of natural rubber or latex,[5] butyl rubber, nitrile rubber, plastic, or rubber-like synthetics such as neoprene.

Keep in mind that these gloves are not uniformly effective against all compounds. Nitrile gloves, for example, are excellent for handling turpentine compounds, which quickly pass through latex gloves.

Carefully review the chemical compositions of the finishes, adhesives, cleaning solvents, and other compounds used at your facility, and provide an array of gloves that offer the necessary protection. In some cases, workers handling multiple chemicals at once may need to wear different gloves in combination.

Chemical resistance specifications for the various glove types are readily available from vendors and manufacturers, as well as directly from OSHA.

Body Protection

You must provide body PPE to those of your employees whose bodies are at risk while performing their tasks. Despite your efforts at hazard mitigation via engineering and work practice controls, some body hazards may continue to exist, including impacts from tools, machinery, and materials; abrasions, lacerations, and allergic dermatitis; splash exposures to hazardous chemicals; and lower back strain. The types of protective garments available to address these hazards include vests, jackets, aprons, overalls, back supports, and full-body suits.

As with gloves, protective clothing for workers operating powered cutting, shaping, and boring equipment should not pose a greater risk than the one being addressed. Avoid loose clothing that could snag in moving parts and pull a worker into harm. Also avoid excessive clothing that could result in reduced mobility or heat exhaustion. Use common sense in your decisionmaking.

---

[5] *Some workers may have or may develop an allergic reaction to latex gloves.*

OSHA offers the following suggestions for selecting appropriate body protection:

• For general impact, abrasion, and laceration protection, heavy leather and/or padded aprons should provide the maximum protection without unnecessarily compromising mobility or ventilation.

• Full-body overalls made of cotton or synthetic fiber should provide adequate protection when engineering controls or worker reassignment cannot prevent allergic reactions to wood dust. The overalls should be snug-fitting to keep out wood dust and other materials that could work their way underneath the fabric and to prevent the fabric from snagging in moving machine parts.

• For chemical splash protection—whether from paints, finishes, adhesives, solvents, or other material—use aprons or full-body suits constructed of suitable barrier material. Rubberized cotton twill aprons or overalls resistant to organic and inorganic chemicals such as high-density polyethylene.

Hearing Protection

You must institute an effective hearing conservation program at your workplace if the engineering controls that you utilize do not lower your employees' daily 8-hour averaged noise exposure to less than 85 dBA. (The section of this guide entitled "What Are My Options for Noise Control?" describes some engineering control options. Note that you must provide hearing protection while such engineering improvements are being made.) OSHA's Occupational Noise Exposure standard,

29 CFR 1910.95, describes the specific procedures that must be included in a hearing conservation program. These include:

• Develop and implement a monitoring program to sample noise levels within the workplace, identify employees for inclusion in the hearing conservation program, and enable the proper selection of hearing protectors.

• Establish and maintain an audiometric testing program in which qualified professionals periodically test the hearing of all workers whose noise exposures equal or exceed a daily 8-hour average of 85 dBA.

• Provide hearing protection, at no charge, to all employees exposed to such levels of noise.

You will likely find that hearing protection will be necessary for most, if not all, of your production employees, as most power woodworking equipment will produce between 100 and 110 dBA of noise at the point of operation, despite any control steps you implement.

The level of protection needed will vary widely for different workers, depending on the duration of their exposure to different noise levels. For example, a full-time band saw operator will probably require more rigorous protection than a general floor worker moving materials between storage, production, and shipping areas. If you employ only a few workers in a small operation, each employee may perform every conceivable task at some point during the work day—a situation which greatly complicates the process of calculating your workers' daily average exposure to noise.

The chapter on noise measurement in the *OSHA Technical Manual* provides specific details on determining your employees' exposure to noise. Appendix B of 29 CFR 1910.95 describes how to determine the level of hearing protection provided by different devices, and how to make appropriate selections based on their noise reduction ratings (NRRs).

> **The general steps to determining the need for hearing PPE for a given worker include**
>
> - Measuring the noise level (dBA) at each work location with a sound level meter and recording the hours per day spent there.
> - Determining the allowable exposure duration limit for the noise level encountered at each location (see Table 4 on page 32).
> - Dividing the amount of time the worker actually spends at each location by the allowable exposure duration limit.
> - Adding the resulting fractions together to compute the equivalent noise factor. Alternately, a noise dosimeter may be used.

If the equivalent noise factor is equal to or greater than 1, you must provide hearing protection. If any one of the factors from an individual location is greater than 1, you must provide protection for that particular task.

Once you have determined the hearing protection needs of your employees, you will have to select appropriate devices. This is a highly important process. Inappropriate hearing protection can isolate individual employees by interfering with effective communication and general workplace awareness. Muffled hearing can cause accidents, render workers unaware of imminent physical hazards, and interfere with coordinated action in the event of an emergency.

Common hearing protection devices include self-forming foam earplugs (disposable or durable), individualized molded earplugs, and earmuffs. Within each category, a variety of products are available, providing varying degrees of noise reduction as measured by their NRRs. You must provide reasonably convenient and comfortable hearing protection to each affected employee so that his or her daily equivalent noise factor is kept below 1. As part of your hearing conservation program, you must also provide training in the use and care of all hearing protection distributed to your employees.

Respiratory Protection

OSHA has specific requirements governing the need for and use of respiratory protection. This guide does not attempt to cover the many detailed topics involved with respiratory protection, such as methods for determining the need for respiratory protection, selecting and purchasing appropriate equipment, training affected workers to use the equipment, and fulfilling the record keeping and medical monitoring requirements.

Respiratory protection may be necessary if any of your employees:

- Suffer from problems associated with wood dust inhalation.
- Routinely handle wood finishes, adhesives, solvents, or other chemical compounds in containers open to the air they breath.
- Work in paint spray booths (or booths where other chemicals are sprayed).

Begin by consulting OSHA Instruction CPL 2-2.54[6] on respiratory protection or contact the nearest OSHA office for assistance.

Once I Have Provided My Employees with the Necessary PPE, Is My Job Done?

No. An effective PPE program means more than simply providing your employees with protective equipment. You should work to create an environment at your facility where the proper and conscientious use of PPE is valued as a vital part of your company's overall commitment to health and safety. In other words, to reap the rewards of your up-front capital investment in PPE, you should be willing to invest your employees' time and effort on a daily basis. Key elements of this ongoing commitment will include training, maintenance (cleaning, repairs, and replacement), and bookkeeping. Consult the OSHA pamphlet *Assessing the Need for Personal Protective Equipment (PPE): A Guide for Small Business Employers* (OSHA 3151) for more discussion on PPE programs.

---

[6] *CPL.2-2.54 is available on OSHA Web page at http://www.osha.gov*

What Are the Hazards of the Chemicals Used in Finishing?

Finishing operations pose a wide range of health and safety hazards due to the volume and physical properties of the chemicals involved. A complete discussion of this topic is beyond the scope of this guide; however, a general discussion of common hazards and related control measures is provided below. To best protect your employees from the chemical hazards related to your finishing operations, you should identify the specific chemicals in use in your facilities and consult the appropriate OSHA standards to determine required controls. See Table 7 at the end of this section for a list of some of the OSHA standards likely to apply to your finishing operations.

Health Hazards

A wide range of adhesives and coating agents are used in finishing wood products. Many of these are hazardous to the health of employees. Chemicals can enter the body in three ways: through inhalation (breathing), ingestion (eating), or contact with the skin. The skin readily absorbs many chemicals, such as solvents, allowing them to enter the bloodstream. Woodworkers are generally exposed to chemicals through inhalation and contact with the skin.

Both nitrocellulose topcoats (lacquers) and acid-catalyzed coatings (conversion varnishes) contain solvents that are toxic to humans. The solvents most commonly used in these coatings include toluene, xylenes, methyl ethyl ketone (MEK), methyl isobutyl ketone (MIBK), and methanol. The acid-catalyzed coatings contain formaldehyde. All of these solvents have short-term effects, such as irritation of the eyes, nose, and throat, and headaches, dizziness, confusion, fatigue, and nausea. The longer-term effects include reproductive problems, central nervous system disorders, and damage to the lungs, liver, and kidneys. Toluene exposure increases the risk of miscarriage. Developmental effects have been noted in children born to mothers who were exposed to toluene and xylenes. Studies have shown that formaldehyde can cause lung and nasal cancer.

Many of the adhesives used in finishing wood products also contain toxic chemicals. The most hazardous are the solvent-based, epoxy resin, and urea-formaldehyde resin adhesives. Many of the solvents used in the coating agents are used in the adhesives. The epoxy resin adhesives are particularly toxic. Methylene chloride, which has been shown to cause cancer in laboratory animals, is often the base for these adhesives. Some of the components of the epoxy resins may also be cancer-causing. Epoxy resin adhesives can also cause dermatitis and a sensitization reaction.

Safety Hazards

In addition to the health hazards posed by the chemicals used in finishing operations, many of the solvents, lacquers, varnishes, and coatings used in these operations are extremely flammable. These materials can pose significant fire and explosion hazards if used in large quantities, in unventilated or enclosed areas, or in processes such as spray finishing operations that can lead to significant airborne concentrations of the material.

How Can I Protect My Employees from the Chemicals Used in Finishing?

Engineering Controls

- When feasible, use automated systems for applying coatings and adhesives. Automated systems should be ventilated.

- Substitute the traditional solvent-based coatings and adhesives with coatings and adhesives that are less toxic. Hot melt, heat seal, aqueous-based, and polyvinyl acetate adhesives are good, less-toxic alternatives to solvent-based adhesives. Higher-solids nitrocellulose, aqueous-based, ultraviolet-cured, and polyester/polyurethane coatings are also less toxic than solvent-based coatings.

- Provide adequate local exhaust ventilation for all coating and gluing processes. This includes manual spray, rolling, and brushing operations, automated coating processes, and dip coating. Manual spray operations should be performed in a spray booth or a separate, ventilated spray

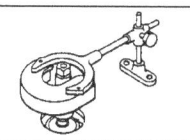

area. Dip coating should be ventilated with an enclosure or capture hood. Consult the OSHA standard on dip coating (open surface tanks), 29 CFR 1910.108, for detailed requirements on dipping operations.

• The OSHA standard for spray finishing operations, 29 CFR 1910.107, provides detailed requirements for the design and construction of spray booths and rooms, air filters, velocity and air flow requirements, and the (make-up) air supplied to the booth. It is important to maintain the proper air flow in a spray booth. Excessive air pressure decreases the efficiency of the operation, wastes material, and may cause a backlash of vapors and overspray into adjacent work areas. Dirty air filters can decrease the air flow in the booth. Ensure that filters are cleaned and replaced as needed. Although these provisions are designed to prevent the occurrence of a fire or explosion in spray finishing operations, they also assist in protecting workers from the health hazards of the chemicals used in the operation by removing the chemicals from the atmosphere.

Controls designed to prevent fire and explosion resulting from the use of flammable and combustible materials in woodworking operations are discussed in the section of this guide entitled, "Is My Facility Susceptible to Fire and Explosion," on page 27. The controls discussed in this section are also generally applicable to your finishing operations. In addition to these controls, however, you should refer to the applicable OSHA standards listed in Table 7 at the end of this section for detailed information on required controls specific to the use of flammable and combustible materials in your finishing operations.

Develop a Hazard Communication or "Right-to-Know" Program

• OSHA's Hazard Communication standard, 29 CFR 1910.1200, requires employers to inform their employees about the hazardous substances they handle. Hazard communication programs have three important components: material safety data sheets (MSDSs), training, and labeling requirements.

MSDSs contain information on the health and safety hazards of chemicals, and recommend appropriate controls. All chemical suppliers must send an MSDS for each chemical a company orders. Employers must make these MSDSs available to employees at all times.

The Hazard Communication standard requires employers to train their employees about the hazards of the chemicals they handle. Employers must train employees upon initial hire, after a transfer, and when new hazardous substances are introduced into the workplace. Employers must keep a written record of the training they provide.

Employers must ensure that all containers are labeled with information about their contents and about the health hazards of the substance.

Personal Protective Equipment

• Provide respirators and gloves for workers performing manual spray operations. Consult the MSDS to determine what type of glove to use. Operators working downstream of the objects being sprayed inside the booth must be provided with an air-supplying respirator. Provide dip-coat operators with gloves, boots, aprons, and jackets, sleeves, or coats to protect them from possible splashes. Consult the MSDS to determine the appropriate material of protective clothing to provide. The "Personal Protective Equipment" section of this guide provides detailed information on PPE requirements.

Other Applicable OSHA Standards

In addition to the Hazard Communication standard discussed above, OSHA has published several standards that may be directly relevant to finishing operations. To determine which of these standards apply to your specific operations, you should consider both the type of chemicals that you will use and how you will use the chemicals. Once you have done this, you should refer to the applicable OSHA standards to determine how to best protect your workers. See Table 7 for OSHA standards particularly relevant to finishing operations.

Table 7. OSHA Standards Relevant to Finishing Operations

- *Ventilation, 29 CFR 1910.94(c) and (d).* These subsections of the standard establish ventilation design requirements for spray finishing and open surface tanks.

- *Flammable and Combustible Liquids, 29 CFR 1910.106.* This standard establishes provisions for the safe handling, storage, and use of flammable and combustible liquids.

- *Spray Finishing Using Flammable and Combustible Materials, 29 CFR 1910.107.* This standard establishes provisions for spray finishing operations using flammable and combustible materials.

- *Dip Tanks Containing Flammable and Combustible Liquids, 29 CFR 1910.108.* This standard establishes provisions for the use of flammable and combustible liquids in dip-tank operations.

- *Respiratory Protection, 29 CFR 1910.134.* This standard establishes minimum requirements for the proper selection, fitting, use, care, storage, and maintenance of respiratory protective equipment.

- *The Air Contaminants standards, 29 CFR 1910.1000.* This standard establishes permissible exposure limits (limits to the airborne concentrations of a specific chemical that workers can be exposed to over a specified period of time) for many of the chemicals used in finishing operations. The standard further establishes general requirements for the use of engineering and administrative controls and personal protective clothing to ensure that workers are not exposed above the established permissible exposure limit.

- *The Methylene Chloride standard, 29 CFR 1910.1052.* This standard establishes specific provisions to protect your workers from exposure to methylene chloride. In addition to establishing permissible exposure limits for methylene chloride, this standard also requires the use of exposure monitoring, regulated areas, engineering and work practice controls, respiratory protection, and medical evaluations.

References

American Conference of Governmental Industrial Hygienists (ACGIH). 1996. *Threshold Limit Values for Chemical Substances and Physical Agents— Biological Exposure Indices.* 6th ed.

ACGIH. *Industrial Ventilation: a Manual of Recommended Practice.* ACGIH Committee on Industrial Ventilation.

Bureau of Labor Statistics. 1995. *Fatal Workplace Injuries in 1993: A Collection of Data and Analysis.* U.S. Department of Labor.

Hampl, V. 1982. *Development of Criteria for Control of Woodworking Operation.* U.S. Department of Health and Human Services. National Institute for Occupational Safety and Health. July.

Firenze, R. J., and J. B. Walters. 1981. *Safety and Health for Industrial/Vocational Education.* U.s. Department of Health and Human Services. July.

Massachusetts Department of Public Health. 1997. Woodworker dies when struck by tool knife launched from overarm router. Occupational Health Surveillance Program. Fatality investigation report 2:2. February.

National Institute for Occupational Safety and Health (NIOSH). 1997. *Questions and Answers: Methylene Chloride Control in Furniture Stripping* (Niosh Publication No. 93-133). U.S. Department of Health and Human Services.

NIOSH. 1975a. *Health and Safety Guide for Wooden Furniture Manufacturing* (NIOSH Publication No. 75-167). U.S. Department of Health and Human Services.

NIOSH. 1975b. Machine guarding—Assessment of need. U.S. Department of Health and Human Services. June.

National Safety Council. 1988. *Accident Prevention Manual for Industrial Operations: Engineering and Technology.* 9th Ed. Itasca, IL: National Safety Council.

National Safety Council. 1993. *Safeguarding Concepts Illustrated.* 6th ed.

Occupational Safety and Health Administration (OSHA). 1997. *Assessing the Need for Personal Protective Equipment (PPE): a Guide for Small Business Employers* (OSHA Publication No. 3151). U.S. Department of Labor.

OSHA. 1992. *Concepts and Techniques of Machine Safeguarding* (OSHA Publication No. 3067). U.S. Department of Labor. See **Index** on OSHA's Website at http://www.osha.gov.

OSHA Standards

Title 29 Code of Federal Regulations (CFR), Part 1910

Subpart D—Walking and Working Surfaces

Subpart E—Means of Egress

Subpart G—Occupational Health and Environmental Control
    1910.94—Ventilation
    1910.95—Noise control

Subpart H—Hazardous Materials
    1910.107—Spray finishing using flammable and combustible materials
    1910.108—Dip tanks containing flammable and combustible materials

Subpart I—Personal Protective Equipment (Covers eye and face, head, foot, hand, and respiratory protection)

Subpart J—General Environmental Controls
    1910.147—Control of hazardous energy ("Lockout Tagout")

Subpart L—Fire Protection

Subpart N—Materials Handling and Storage
    1910.178—Powered industrial trucks

Subpart O—Machinery and Machine Guarding
    1910.212—General requirements for all machines

1910.213—Woodworking machinery requirements
1910.219—Mechanical power transmission apparatus

Subpart S—Electrical

Subpart Z—Toxic and Hazardous Substances
1910.1200—Hazard communication

Other Standards

National Fire Protection Association:

NFPA 10	Installation of Portable Fire Extinguishers
NFPA 33	Standard for Spray Finishing Using Flammable and Combustible Materials
NFPA 70	National Electrical Code
NFPA 644-1993	Standard for the Prevention of Fires and Explosions in Wood Processing and Woodworking Facilities

American National Standards Institute:

ANSI Z9.2	Fundamentals Governing the Design and Operation of Local Exhaust Systems
ANSI O1.1-1992	Woodworking Machinery - Safety Requirements

The National Institute for Occupational safety and Health (NIOSH) has published a series of seven *Hazard Controls* fact sheets concerning wood dust control techniques. In this Appendix, NIOSH articles on controlling dust from woodworking machineries are consolidated for use as applicable. NIOSH is the federal agency responsible for conducting research and making recommendations for preventing work-related illness and injuries. *Hazard Controls* are based on research studies that show reduced worker exposure to hazardous agents or activities. Copies of the *Hazard Controls* fact sheets and additional information about hazard control can be obtained by calling **NIOSH at 1-800-35-NIOSH** or visiting NIOSH's website at www.cdc.gov/niosh/publistd.html. The following is a list of NIOSH's *Hazard Controls* covered in this Appendix.

Control of Wood Dust from Horizontal Belt Sanders, DHHS (NIOSH) Publication No. 96-121.

Control of Wood Dust from Shapers, DHHS (NIOSH) Publication No. 96-122.

Control of Wood Dust from Automated Routers, DHHS (NIOSH) Publication No. 96-123.

Control of Wood Dust from Large Diameter Disc Sanders, DHHS (NIOSH) Publication No. 96-124.

Control of Wood Dust from Random Orbital Hand Sanders, DHHS (NIOSH) Publication No. 96-125.

Control of Wood Dust from Orbital Hand Sanders, DHHS (NIOSH) Publication No. 96-126.

Control of Wood Dust from Table Saws, DHHS (NIOSH) Publication No. 96-127.

Control of Wood Dust from Horizontal Belt Sanders

Hazard

The use of horizontal belt sanders in woodworking creates significant amounts of wood dust. Workers exposed to wood dusts have experienced a variety of adverse health effects such as eye and skin irritation, allergy, reduced lung function, asthma, and nasal cancer. NIOSH, therefore, recommends limiting wood dust exposures to prevent these health problems.

Controls

Surveys by NIOSH researchers indicated that wood dust from the horizontal belt sanders used in woodworking was not effectively controlled. As a result, researchers developed an inexpensive auxiliary ventilation system for the horizontal belt sanders that significantly reduced wood dust emissions into the workroom.

• Auxiliary Ventilation System

Typically, belt sander emissions are controlled only by an exhaust hood covering the drive pulley. The new ventilation system reduced wood dust emitted into the workroom by more than 75% and can easily be built into new belt sanders or added to existing ones. The system consists of two devices: a narrow Auxiliary Hood and an Air Jet Stripper (see Figure 25). The Auxiliary Hood is located between the belt surface and the worktable downstream from the sanding operation. The Air Jet Stripper is located inside the main exhaust hood. These two devices, in combination with the main exhaust hood, decrease wood dust in the workroom without affecting the sanding operations. In addition, the Jet Stripper cleans the belt, reducing the frequency of belt changes. This dust control device is not currently commercially available.

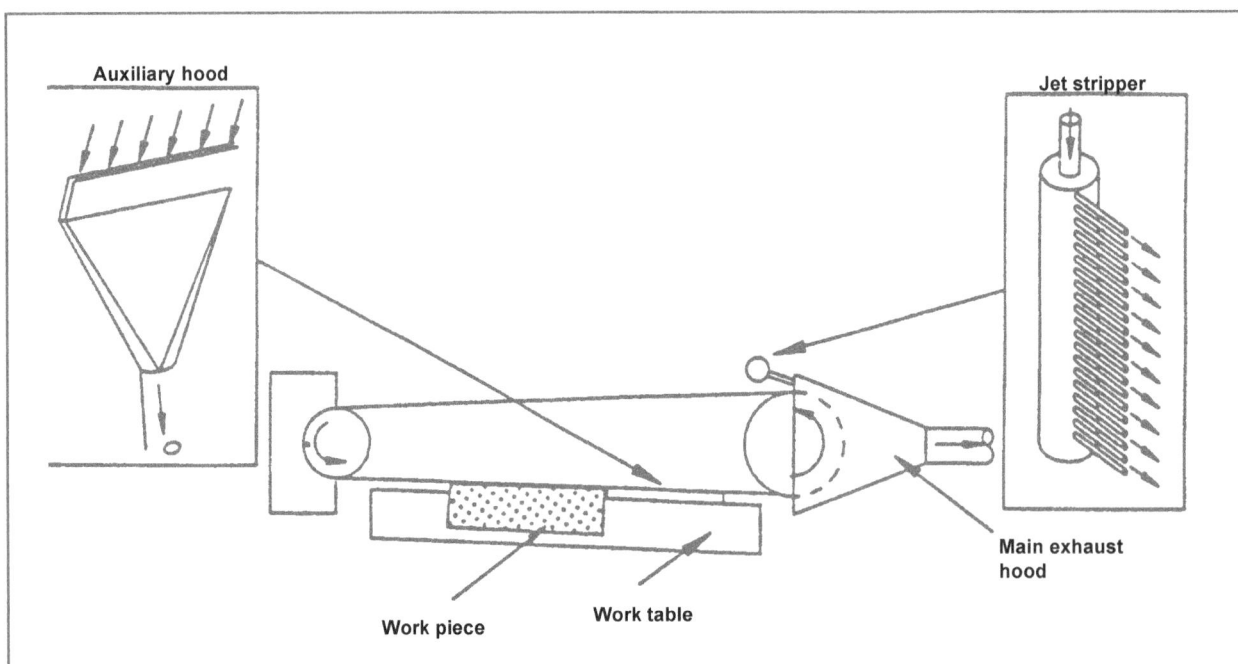

Figure 25. Auxiliary Ventilation System for Horizontal Belt Sanders

Control of Wood Dust from Shapers

Hazard

Wood shapers are a major source of wood dust emissions. Workers exposed to wood dusts have experienced a variety of adverse health effects such as eye and skin irritation, allergy, reduced lung function, asthma, and nasal cancer. NIOSH, therefore, recommends limiting wood dust exposures to prevent these health problems.

Controls

Surveys by NIOSH researchers found that the dust from wood shapers tends to be poorly controlled. The amount of wood dust emitted was found to depend on the sharpness of the cutter, the depth of the cut, the rate at which the wood is fed into the shaper, and the location of the exhaust hood. After studying the usual hood exhaust placement, researchers developed an improved hood configuration that significantly reduced wood dust emissions.

• Modified Exhaust Hood

Wood shaper emissions are usually controlled by an exhaust hood located at the back edge of the work table which allows the operator to freely move the workpiece over the table. Placing the exhaust hood nearer the cutting head would maximize dust collection, however, this would restrict the operator's freedom to move the workpiece. To overcome this problem, a hood extension with a flexible face opening is added (see Figure 26). The flexible face opening consists of cloth-covered chains that allow the wood to pass through, but stops the wood dust particles. The extension also increases the hood face velocity by minimizing the open face area. This dust control device is not currently commercially available.

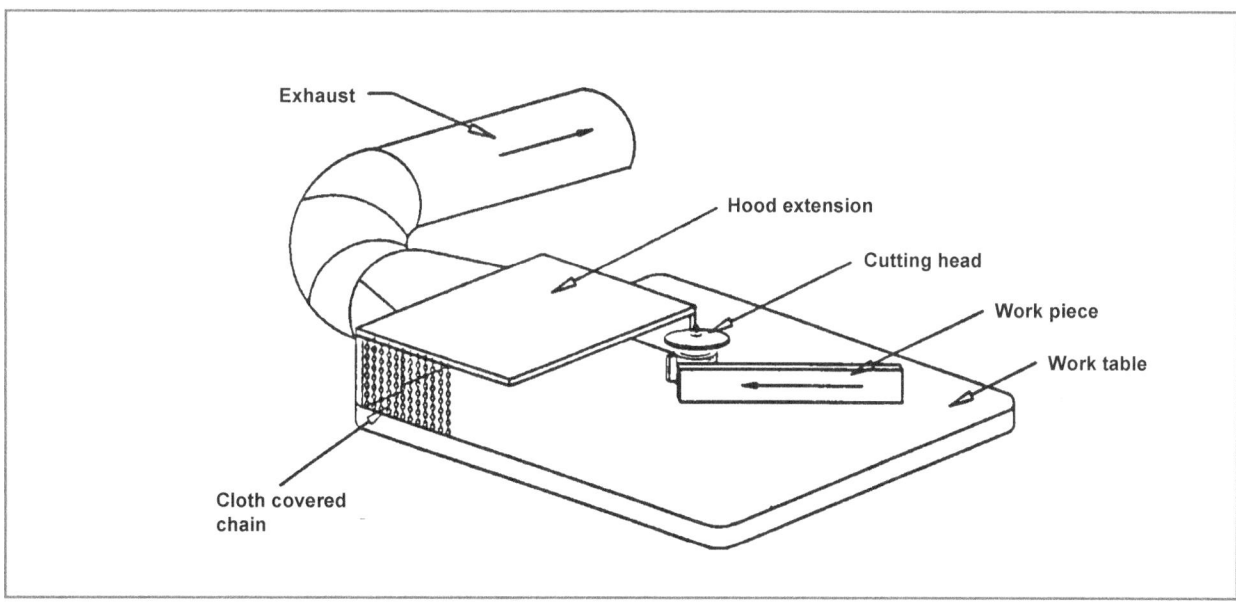

Figure 26. Improved Hood Configuration for Shapers

Control of Wood Dust from Automated Routers

Hazard

Automated routers have been found to create significant amounts of wood dust. Workers exposed to wood dusts have experienced a variety of adverse health effects such as eye and skin irritation, allergy, reduced lung function, asthma, and nasal cancer. NIOSH, therefore, recommends limiting wood dust exposures to prevent these health problems.

Controls

NIOSH researchers found that the wood dust generated by automated routers is generally not adequately controlled. To address this problem, researchers designed and tested a new control system that substantially reduced dust emissions.

• **Jet Stripper System**

Automated routers, consisting of a moving router head and table, are capable of routing in any direction. These high speed machines generate substantial amounts of wood dust. Generally, the wood dust is controlled by a local exhaust system located at the router head. Despite this control, significant amounts of wood dust are emitted into the workroom. A computer controlled Jet Stripper System was developed to control these emissions (see Figure 27). This system consists of 24 jets combined into 8 operational units uniformly located around the inside periphery of the brush holder. The Jet Stripper and brush surround the router bit. The jets are supplied with pressurized air and are activated by pneumatic valves as needed. The air slows down the dust particles so they can be collected by the local exhaust hood. Testing shows that this system reduces wood dust emissions by 90 percent. The Jet Stripper does not interfere with the operator, requires minimal maintenance and is inexpensive to install and operate. This control can also be used with conventional, one-dimensional routers with some modification. This dust control device is not currently commercially available.

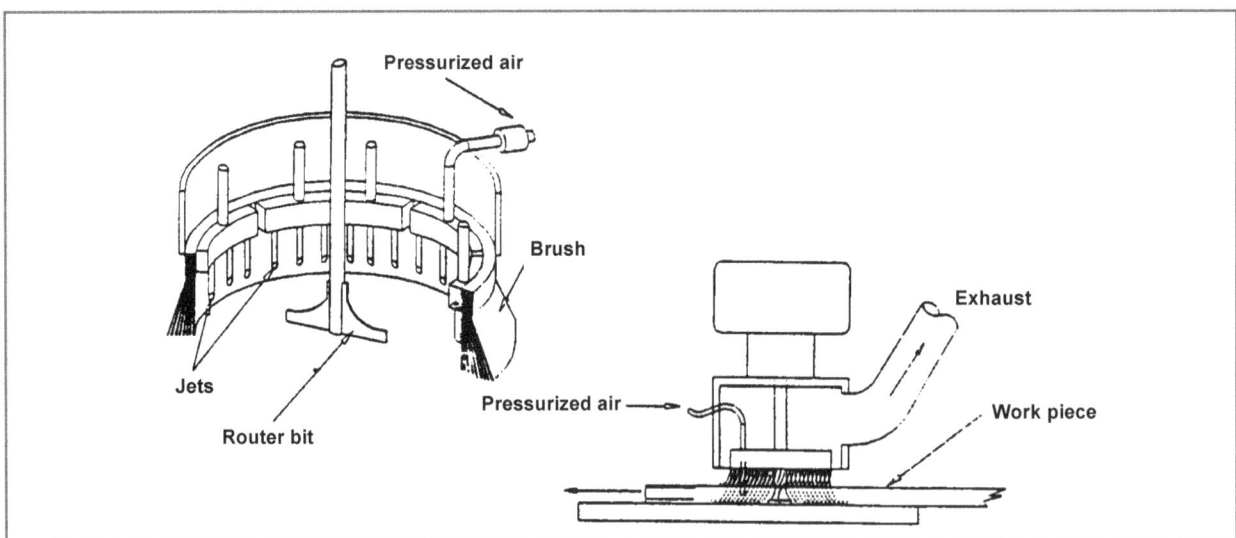

Figure 27. Computer-Controlled Jet Stripper System for Controlling Emissions from Automated Routers

Control of Wood Dust from Large Diameter Disc Sanders

Hazard

The use of large diameter disc sanders creates significant amounts of wood dust. Workers exposed to wood dusts have experienced a variety of adverse health effects such as eye and skin irritation, allergy, reduced lung function, asthma, and nasal cancer. NIOSH, therefore, recommends limiting wood dust exposures to prevent these health problems.

Controls

Surveys by NIOSH researchers found that wood dust created by large diameter disc sanders is often not effectively controlled. To address this problem, researchers designed a ventilation control system that significantly reduced wood dust emissions into the workroom.

• Jetstripper System

The standard dust control arrangement for disc sanders usually consists of an exhaust hood under the worktable that covers the lower half of the disc and a cover around the back of the sanding disc above the worktable. Even with this control, significant amounts of wood dust are emitted into the workroom. A Jet Stripper System was designed to improve dust control (see Figure 28). The Jet Stripper supplies pressurized air to the disc inside the hood. The jet of high speed air blows the dust particles out of the disc air layer so they can be captured by the exhaust hood. Also, the jet removes the dust particles embedded in the sanding disc. The Jet Stripper System reduced wood dust emissions by an average of 60 percent in laboratory studies. The advantages of this control are that it does not interfere with the operator, requires minimal maintenance and is inexpensive to operate. The Jet Stripper may also extend the life of the sanding discs by dislodging the wood dust from the sanding surface. This dust control device is not currently commercially available.

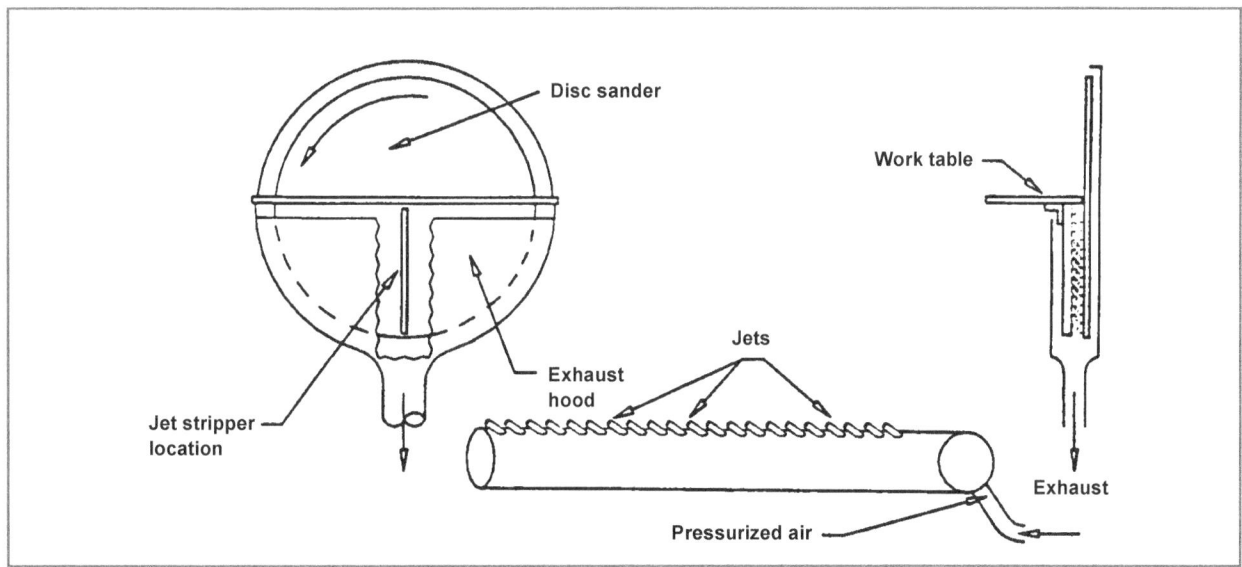

Figure 28. Jet Stripper System for Improving Dust Control from Disc Sanders

Control of Wood Dust from Random Orbital Hand Sanders

Hazard

Random orbital (rotating) hand sanders have been found to create significant amounts of wood dust. Workers exposed to wood dusts have experienced a variety of adverse health effects such as eye and skin irritation, allergy, reduced lung function, asthma, and nasal cancer. NIOSH, therefore, recommends limiting wood dust exposures to prevent these health problems.

Controls

NIOSH researchers found that wood dust created by random orbital hand sanders is often poorly controlled. To address this problem, researchers designed and tested a new control system for these hand sanders that significantly reduced dust emissions.

• Additional Exhaust System

Random orbital hand sanders are widely used in woodworking applications. The dust generated by these tools is sometimes controlled by an aspirator in combination with a perforated sanding pad. The aspirator creates a vacuum to draw wood dust up through holes in the sanding pad. It was found that, in spite of this control, large amounts of wood dust were still emitted into the workroom. A new control system that uses Additional Exhaust and a Slotted Sanding Pad was implemented to increase dust control (see Figure 29). The increased suction of the additional exhaust alone causes the sanding pad to be pulled to the work surface making the tool difficult to use. To alleviate this problem, curved slots are cut into the sanding pad. This relieves the pressure caused by the extra suction and provides additional dust control at the pad periphery. The new dust control system reduces dust emissions by approximately 90 percent compared with the currently used aspirator controlled sander. The new sander does not interfere with the operator, requires no special maintenance and is inexpensive to operate. This dust control device is not currently commercially available.

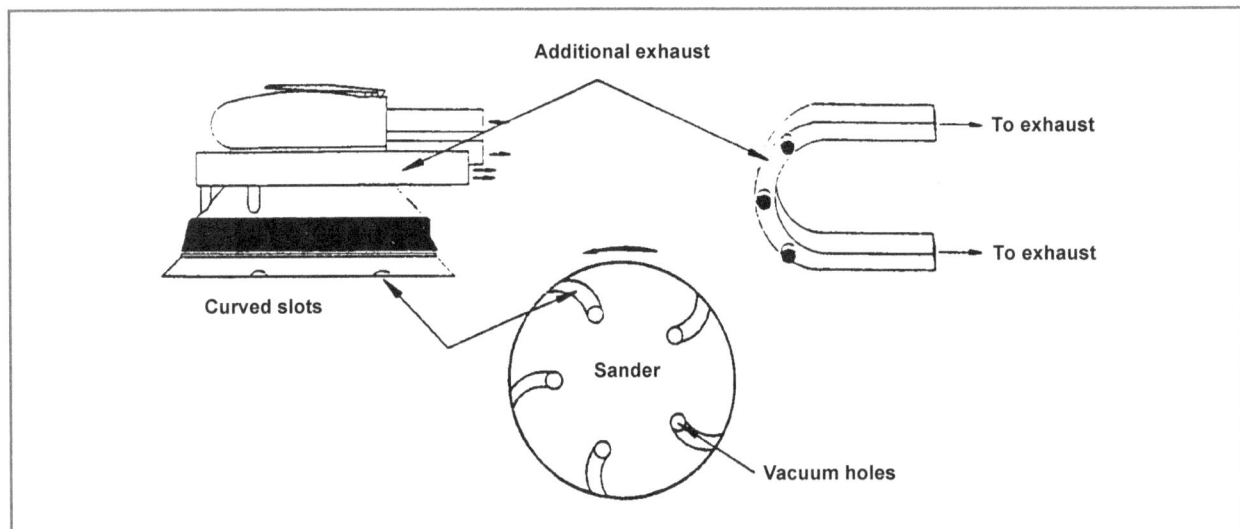

Figure 29. Dust Control System for Random Orbital Hand Sanders

Control of Wood Dust from Orbital Hand Sanders

Hazard

Orbital hand sanders have been found to create significant amounts of wood dust. Workers exposed to wood dusts have experienced a variety of adverse health effects such as eye and skin irritation, allergy, reduced lung function, asthma, and nasal cancer. NIOSH, therefore, recommends limiting wood dust exposures to prevent these health problems.

Controls

NIOSH researchers found that the wood dust generated by orbital hand sanders is often poorly controlled. To address this problem, researchers designed and tested a new control system for these hand sanders that significantly reduced dust emissions.

• Dust Control System

Orbital hand sanders are extensively used in woodworking processes. The dust from these sanders is generally not controlled although some are equipped with dust removal capabilities. However, even the sanders having dust removal do not effectively control the wood dust generated by the sanding operation. Therefore, a new control approach was developed. A Dust Control Plenum was designed and tested on an orbital sander (see Figure 30). The plenum fits between the sanding pad and the sander body and has a series of exhaust slots along its edges. An exhaust connection on the top of the sander pad connects the plenum with a vacuum source. Laboratory tests show that the plenum reduces wood dust emissions by approximately 90 percent. The plenum does not interfere with the operator's activities, requires no special maintenance, is inexpensive to operate, and can be used on any sander, pneumatically or electrically powered. This dust control device is not currently commercially available. Call NIOSH for more information.

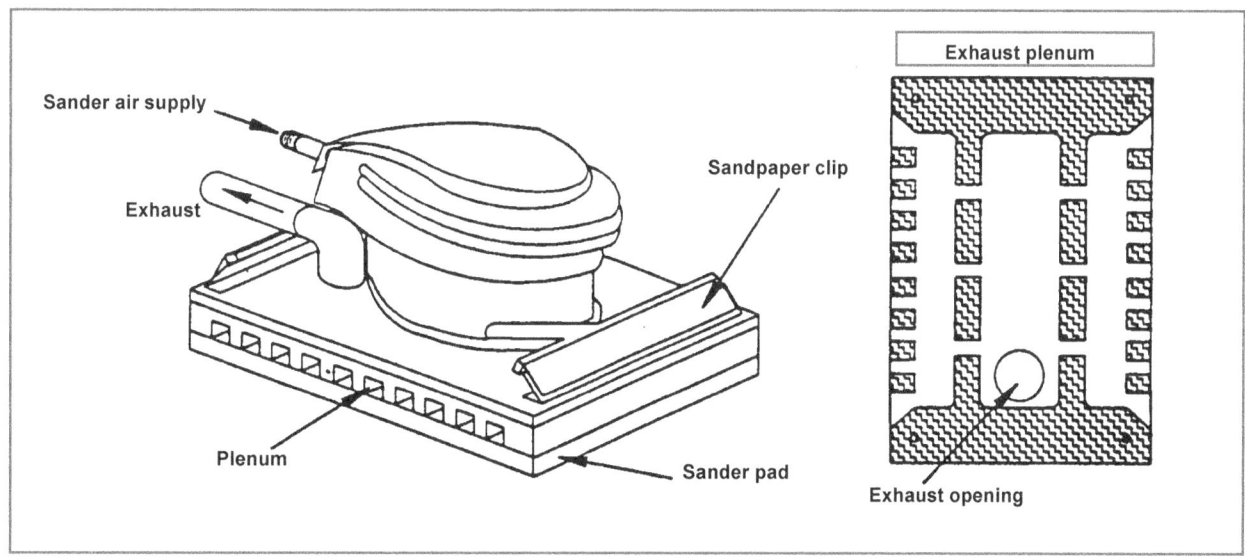

Figure 30. Dust Control Plenum for Orbital Hand Sanders

Control of Wood Dust from Table Saws

Hazard

Table saws have been found to create significant amounts of wood dust. Workers exposed to wood dusts have experienced a variety of adverse health effects such as eye and skin irritation, allergy, reduced lung function, asthma, and nasal cancer. NIOSH recommends limiting wood dust exposures to prevent these health problems.

Controls

NIOSH researchers found that the wood dust generated by table saws is often poorly controlled. To address this problem, researchers designed and tested a control system for table saws that significantly reduced wood dust emissions.

• Local Exhaust Hood

Table saws are widely used in many types of woodworking operations. Although they are sometimes used only sporadically, they are found to generate significant amounts of dust. The traditional method of dust control for table saws is exhaust through the bottom of the table. This is often not adequate to control the large amounts of high speed dust that are generated by the saw blade. To better control the dust, NIOSH researchers added a Local Exhaust Hood to the table saw (see Figure 31). Another modification involved the addition of a divider plate in the table base to increase the exhaust velocity and aid clean out. The table exhaust location was also relocated. The exhaust hood, when placed over the top of the blade saw, contains the dust as it is thrown from the saw blade. Laboratory testing indicates that the exhaust hood reduces wood dust emissions by greater than 90 percent when it is installed on a typical table saw. The hood is designed so that it will not interfere with the operator's activities, is easy to install and maintain, and is inexpensive to operate. This dust control device is not currently commercially available.

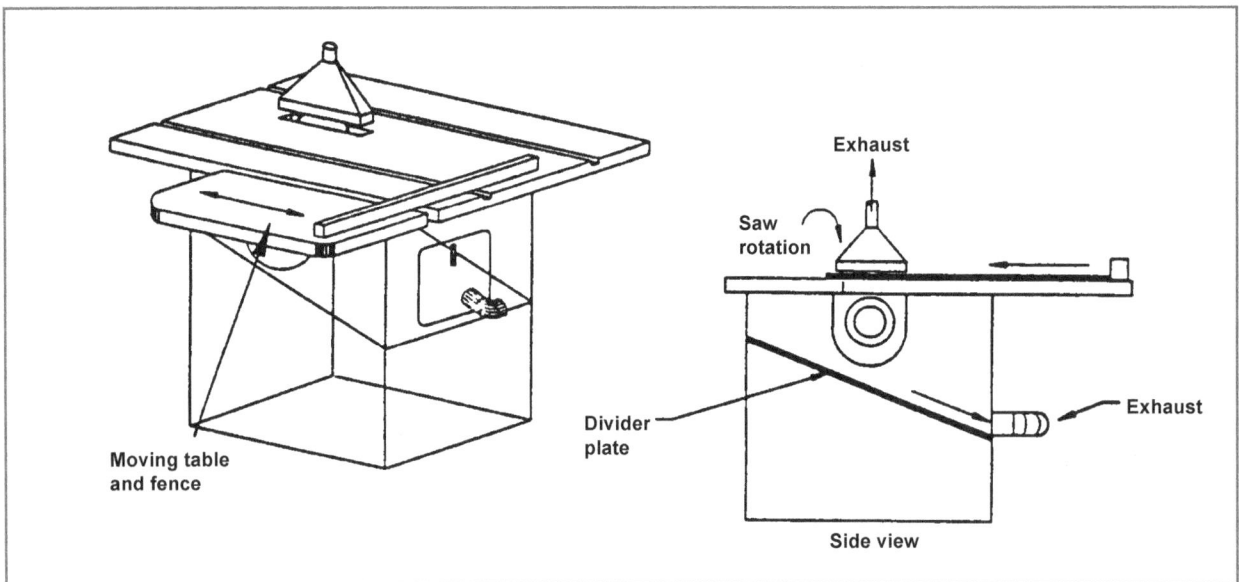

Figure 31. Local Exhaust Hood for Table Saws

State and Local Government Resources

Several states have developed relevant requirements, guidelines, or recommendations. These include California OSHA, *CAL/OSHA Guidelines for Workplace Security,* and *Model Injury and Illness Prevention Program for Workplace Security;* the State of Florida, *Convenience Business Security Act, and Study of Safety and Security Requirements for "At-Risk" Businesses;* the State of Virginia, *Report to the Virginia State Crime Commission on Violent Crime and Workers' Safety in Virginia Convenience Stores;* and *Violent Crimes in Convenient Stores: Analysis of Crimes, Criminals, and Costs;* and the State of Washington Department of Labor and Industries, *Violence in Washington Workplaces, and Late Night Retail Workers' Crime Protection.* Information is available from these and other agencies to assist employers who are trying to implement an effective workplace violence prevention program. (See also Selected Bibliography.)

Sources of OSHA Assistance

OSHA has a variety of products and programs available to help employers comply with its regulations and improve workplace safety and health. These include numerous publications on regulatory topics, such as hazard communication, asbestos, bloodborne pathogens, and on programs such as consultation, voluntary protection, grants, and training and education to name a few.

Publications are available either as a single free copy per request or for sale by the U.S. Government Printing Office. Lists of publications are available from the OSHA Publications Office, P.O. Box 37535, Washington, DC 20013-7535, (202) 693-1888 (phone); (202) 693-2498 (fax). OSHA also has several videos available on loan or for sale by National Technical Information Service (http://www.ntis.gov) and its National Audiovisual Service (see OSHA publication 2019).

OSHA also offers a variety of programs and initiatives to help employers comply with the agency's standards or guidelines, as discussed in the following paragraphs.

Safety and Health Program Management Guidelines

A single free copy of the guidelines can be obtained from the OSHA Publications Office, P.O. Box 37535, Washington, DC 20013-7535 by sending a self-addressed label with your request or by calling (202) 219-4667. The guidelines are also available on OSHA's web site at http://www.osha.gov/under **Federal Register Notices.**

State Programs

Many states have their own OSHA-approved safety and health regulations covering workplaces in their jurisdiction. *The Occupational Safety and Health Act of 1970* encourages states to develop and operate their own job safety and health plans. States with plans approved under section 18(b) of the *OSH Act* must adopt standards and enforce requirements that are at least as effective as federal requirements.

There are currently 25 state plan states: 23 covering private and public (state and local government) sectors and two covering public sector only. Plan states must adopt standards comparable to the federal within 6 months of a federal standard's promulgation. Until such time as a state standard is promulgated, Federal OSHA provides interim enforcement assistance, as appropriate, in these states.

A listing of the state plan states appears on the Home Page at http://www.osha.gov/under **Office Directory**; an explanation appears under Programs and Services. See also the enclosed list of **States with Approved Plans** at the end of this appendix.

Consultation Program

Another way OSHA helps employers, especially small employers, is through its consultation program. Free onsite safety and health consultation services are available to employers in all states who want help in establishing and maintaining a safe and healthful workplace. Largely funded by OSHA and primarily developed for smaller employers with more hazardous operations, state governments employing professional safety and health consultants provide the consultation service, on request, to those employers who ask for help. These consultants offer employers comprehensive assistance that includes an appraisal of all mechanical systems, physical work practices, and environmental hazards of the workplace and all aspects of the employer's present job safety and health program.

This program is completely separate from the OSHA inspection efforts. No penalties are proposed or citations issued for any safety or health problems identified by the consultant. The service is confidential.

Another incentive program, SHARP (Safety and Health Achievement Recognition Program), recognizes employers with comprehensive, effective safety and health programs. SHARP is open to small high-hazard employers to do the following:

- request full-service consultation assistance;
- involve their employees in the development, operation, and improvement of all elements of the program;
- work with project consultants for at least one year to improve worker protection at the site; and
- meet other program requirements.

In return, employers receive public recognition for exemplary efforts and achievement, reap the benefits of extensive professional assistance, and may be eligible to receive a 1-year exemption from OSHA general scheduled inspections.

For more information concerning consultation services, see **Programs and Services** and the list of consultation projects under **Office Directory** on OSHA's Home Page, or the Consultation Project Directory in Appendix D.

Voluntary Protection Programs

OSHA's Voluntary Protection Programs (VPP) also help employers and employees recognize and promote effective safety and health program management. In the VPP, management, labor, and OSHA establish cooperative relationships at workplaces that have implemented strong programs.

Sites approved for VPP's *Star, Merit,* and *Demonstration* programs have met—and must continue meeting—rigorous participation standards. Benefits of VPP participation include improved employee motivation to work safely, leading to better quality and productivity; lost-workday case rates that generally are 60 to 80 percent below industry averages; reduced workers' compensation and other injury- and illness-related costs; positive community recognition and interaction; further improvement and revitalization for already good safety and health programs; and partnership with OSHA.

For additional information about the VPP, contact the VPP Manager in your nearest OSHA regional office listed under **Office Directory** on OSHA's Home Page or see the lists of OSHA Regional and Area Offices at the end of this appendix.

Training and Education

OSHA's area offices offer a variety of information services, such as publications, audiovisual aids, technical advice, and speakers for special engagements. OSHA's Training Institute in Des Plaines, IL, provides basic and advanced courses in safety and health for federal and state compliance officers, state consultants, federal agency personnel, and private sector employers, employees, and their representatives. To meet the demand for these courses, OSHA also has 12 Training Institute Education Centers nationwide. These centers—comprised of nonprofit colleges, universities, and other organizations— offer a variety of OSHA courses for private and federal sectors.

OSHA also provides funds to nonprofit organizations, through grants, to conduct workplace training and education in subjects where OSHA believes there is a lack of workplace training. Grants are awarded annually. Grant recipients are expected to contribute 20 percent of the total grant cost.

For more information on grants, training, and education, contact the OSHA Training Institute, Office of Training and Education, 1555 Times Drive, Des Plaines, IL 60018, phone (847) 297-4810 or fax (847) 297-4874. See also **Programs and Services,** *Training and Education,* on OSHA's Home Page.

Electronic Information

Internet—OSHA standards, interpretations, directives, publications, and additional information are available or can be ordered online from OSHA's Home Page at http://www.osha.gov/.

For example, to search for OSHA standards, go to the OSHA Home Page and select **Standards,** or **Federal Register Notices.** For information on specific chemicals or substances, go to **Technical Information.** See also categories on **Compliance Assistance, Programs and Services,** and **OSHA Software/Advisors.** All categories allow search functions to help you locate the information you need.

CD-ROM—A wide variety of OSHA materials including standards, interpretations, directives, and more can be purchased on CD-ROM from the Government Printing Office. To order, write to Superintendent of Documents, P.O. Box 371954, Pittsburgh, PA 15250-7954. Specify *OSHA Regulations, Documents, and Technical Information* on CD-ROM, (ORDT); S/N 729-013-00000-5. The price is $38 per year (4 discs quarterly); single copy $15. (Foreign costs: $47.50 annually; $18.75 single copy.)

In addition, OSHA has interactive compliance assistance software, *OSHA Expert Systems,* or *Advisors,* to help responde to individual compliance questions. These deal with confined spaces, asbestos, and cadmium. A new test version on fire safety also is available. These can be downloaded from OSHA's Home Page under **OSHA Software/ Advisors.**

Emergencies

To report life-threatening situations, catastrophes, or fatalities, call **(800) 321-OSHA.** Complaints will go immediately to the nearest OSHA area or state office for help.

You can also contact your nearest OSHA area or regional office listed in Appendix D or online under **Office Directory** on OSHA's Home Page.

Sates with Approved Plans

Commissioner
Alaska Department of Labor
1111 West 8th Street
P.O. Box 24119
Room 306
Juneau, AK 99802-1149
(907) 465-2700

Director
Industrial Commissioner of Arizona
800 W. Washington
Phoenix, AZ 85007
(602) 542-5795

Director
California Department of Industrial Relations
45 Fremont Street
San Francisco, CA 94105
(415) 972-8835

Commissioner
Connecticut Department of Labor
200 Folly Brook Boulevard
Wethersfield, CT 06109
(860) 566-5123

Director
Connecticut Department of Labor
38 Wolcott Hill Road
Wethersfield, CT 06109
(860) 566-4550

Director
Hawaii Department of Labor
and Industrial Relations
830 Punchbowl Street
Honolulu, HI 96813
(808) 586-8844

Commissioner
Indiana Department of Labor
State Office Building
402 West Washington Street
Room W195
Indianapolis, IN 46204
(317) 232-2378

Commissioner
Iowa Division of Labor Services
1000 E. Grand Avenue
Des Moines, IA 50319
(515) 281-3447

Secretary
Kentucky Labor Cabinet
1047 U.S. Highway, 127 South
Suite 2, Frankfort, KY 40601
(502) 564-3070

Commissioner
Maryland Division of Labor and Industry
Department of Labor Licensing and Regulation
1100 N. Eutaw Street, Room 613
Baltimore, MD 21201-2206
(410) 767-2292

Director
Michigan Department of Consumer
and Industry Services
4th Floor, Law Building
P.O. Box 30004
Lansing, MI 48909
(517) 373-7230

Commissioner
Minnesota Department of Labor and Industry
443 Lafayette Road
St. Paul, MN 55155
(612) 296-2342

Director
Nevada Division of Industrial Relations
400 West King Street
Carson City, NV 89703
(702) 687-3032

Secretary
New Mexico Environment Department
1190 St. Francis Drive
P.O. Box 26110
Santa Fe, NM 87502
(505) 827-2850

Commissioner
New York Department of Labor
W. Averell Harriman State Office
Building - 12, Room 500
Albany, NY 12240
(518) 457-2741

Commissioner
North Carolina Department of Labor
4 West Edenton Street
Raleigh, NC 27601-1092
(919) 807-2900

Administrator
Department of Consumer and Business Services
Occupational Safety and Health
  Division (OR-OSHA)
350 Winter Street, NE, Room 430
Salem, OR 97310-0220
(503) 378-3272

Secretary
Puerto Rico Department of Labor
  and Human Resources
Prudencio Rivera Martinez Building
505 Munoz Rivera Avenue
Hato Rey, PR 00918
(787) 754-2119

Commissioner
South Carolina Department of Labor
Licensing and Regulation
110 Centerview Drive
P.O. Box 11329
Columbia, SC 29210
(803) 896-4300

Commissioner
Tennessee Department of Labor
710 James Robertson Parkway
Nashville, TN 37243-0659
(615) 741-2582

Commissioner
Labor Commission of Utah
160 East 300 South, 3rd Floor
P.O. Box 146600
Salt Lake City, UT 84114-6650
(801) 530-6880

Commissioner
Vermont Department of Labor and Industry
National Life Building - Drawer 20
120 State Street
Montpelier, VT 05620-3401
(802) 828-2288

Commissioner
Virginia Department of Labor and Industry
Powers-Taylor Building
13 South 13th Street
Richmond, VA 23219
(804) 786-2377

Commissioner
Virgin Islands Department of Labor
16-AB Church Street
St. Croix, VI 00820-4666
(340) 773-1994

Director
Washington Department of Labor and Industries
General Administrative Building
P.O. Box 44001
Olympia, WA 98504-4001
(360) 902-4200

Administrator
Worker's Safety and Compensation
  Division (WSC)
Wyoming Department of Employment
Herschler Building, 2nd Floor East
122 West 25th Street
Cheyenne, WY 82002
(307) 777-7786

OSHA Consultation Project Directory

Alabama
Safety State Program University of Alabama
425 Martha Parham West
P.O. Box 870388
Tuscaloosa, AL 35487
(205) 348-7136

Alaska
Division of Consultation and Training
ADOL/OSHA
3301 Eagle Street, Suite 305
P.O. Box 107022
Anchorage, AK 99510
(907) 269-4957

Arizona
Consultation and Training
Division of Occupational Safety and Health
Industrial Commission of Arizona
800 West Washington
Phoenix, AZ 85007-9070
(602) 542-5795

Arkansas
OSHA Consultation
Arkansas Department of Labor
10421 West Markham
Little Rock, AK 72205
(501) 682-4522

California
CAL/OSHA Consultation Service
Department of Industrial Relations
45 Freemont Street, Room 5346
San Francisco, CA 94105
(415) 972-8515

Colorado
Occupational Safety and Health Section
Colorado State University
115 Environmental Health Building
Fort Collins, CO 80523
(970) 491-6151

Connecticut
Division of Occupational Safety and Health
Connecticut Department of Labor
38 Wolcott Hill Road
Wethersfield, CT 06109
(860) 566-4550

Delaware
Occupational Safety and Health
Division of Industrial Affairs
Delaware Department of Labor
4425 Market Street
Wilmington, DE 19802
(302) 761-8219

District of Columbia
Office of Occupational Safety and Health
D. C. Department of Employment Services
950 Upshur Street, N.W.
Washington, D.C. 20011
(202) 576-6339

Florida
7(c)(1) Onsite Consultation Program
Division of Safety
Florida Department of Labor and Employment
  Security
2002 St. Augustine Road
Building E, Suite 45
Tallahassee, FL 32399-0663
(904) 488-3044

Georgia
7(c)(1) Onsite Consultation Program
Georgia Institute of Technology
O'Keefe Building, Room 22
Atlanta, GA 30332
(404) 894-2643

Guam
OSHA Onsite Consultation
Department of Labor, Government of Guam
P. O. Box 9970
Tamuning, Guam 96931
(671) 475-0136

Hawaii

Consultation and Training Branch
Department of Labor and Industrial Relations
830 Punchbowl Street
Honolulu, HI 96831
(808) 586-9100

Idaho

Safety and Health Consultation Program
Boise State University
Department of Health Studies
1910 University Drive, ET-338A
Boise, ID 83752
(208) 385-3283

Illinois

Illinois Onsite Consultation
Industrial Service Division
Department of Commerce and Community Affairs
State of Illinois Center
100 West Randolph Street, Suite 3-400
Chicago, IL 60601
(312) 814-2337

Indiana

Division of Labor
Bureau of Safety, Education, and Training
402 West Washington, Room W195
Indianapolia, IN 46204-2287
(317) 232-2688

Iowa

7(c)(1) Consultation Program
Iowa Bureau of Labor
1000 East Grand Avenue
Des Moines, IA 50319
(515) 965-7162

Kansas

Kansas 7(c)(1) Consultation Program
Kansas Department of Human Resources
512 South West 6th Street
Topeka, KS 66603-3150
(913) 296-7476

Kentucky

Division of Education and Training
Kentucky Labor Cabinet
1047 U.S. Highway 127, South
Frankfort, KY 40601
(502) 564-6895

Louisiana

7(c)(1) Consultation Program
Louisiana Department of Labor
P.O. Box 94094
Baton Rouge, LA 70804-9094
(504) 342-9601

Maine

Division of Industrial Safety
Maine Bureau of Labor Standards
Workplace Safety and Health Division
State House Station #82
Augusta, ME 04333
(207) 624-6460

Maryland

Division of Labor and Industry
312 Marshall Avenue, Room 600
Laurel, MD 20707
(410) 880-4970

Massachusetts

The Commonwealth of Massachusetts
Department of Labor and Industries
1001 Watertown Street
West Newton, MA 02165
(617) 727-3982

Michigan (Health)

Department of Consumer and Industry Services
Divison of Occupational Health
3423 North Martin Luther King, Jr. Boulevard
Lansing, MI 48909
(517) 322-1817 (H)

Michigan (Safety)

Department of Consumer and Industry Services
Bureau of Safety and Regulation
7150 Harris Drive
Lansing, MI 48909
(517) 322-1809 (S)

Minnesota
Department of Labor and Industry
Conultation Divison
433 LaFayette Road
Saint Paul, MN 55155
(612) 297-2393

Mississippi
Mississippi State University
Center for Safety and Health
2906 North State Street
Sutie 201
Jackson, MS 39216
(601) 987-3981

Missouri
Onsite Consultation Program
Division of Labor Standards
Department of Labor and Industrial Relations
3315 West Truman Boulevard
P.O. Box 449
Jefferson City, MO 65109
(573) 751-3403

Montana
Department of Labor and Industry
Bureau of Safety
P.O. Box 1728
Helena, MT 59624-1728
(406) 444-6418

Nebraska
Division of Safety Labor and Safety Standards
Nebraska Department of Labor
State Office Building, Lower level
301 Centennial Mall, South
Lincoln, NE 68509-5024
(402) 471-4717

Nevada
Division of Preventive Safety
Department of Industrial Relations
2500 West Washington, Suite 106
Las Vegas, NV 89106
(702) 486-5016

New Hampshire
New Hampshire Department of Health
Divison of Public Health Services
6 Hazen Drive
Concord, NH 03301-6527
(603) 271-2024

New Jersey
Divison of Public Safety and Occupational
    Safety and Health
New Jersey Department of Labor
225 East State Street, 8th Floor West
P.O. Box 953
Trenton, NJ 08625-0953
(609) 292-3923

New Mexico
New Mexico Environment Department
Occupational Health and Safety Bureau
525 Camino de los Marquez, Suite 3
P.O. Box 26110
Santa Fe, NM 87501
(505) 827-4230

New York
Division of Safety and Health
State Office Campus
Building 12, Room 130
Albany, NY 12240
(518) 457-1169

North Carolina
Bureau of Consultative Services
North Carolina Department of Labor-OSHA
319 Chapanoke Road, Suite 105
Raleigh, NC 27603-3432
(919) 662-4644

North Dakota
Division of Environmental Engineering
1200 Missouri Avenue, Room 304
Bismarck, ND 58504
(701) 328-5188

Ohio
Division of Onsite Consultation
Bureau of Employment Services
145 S. Front Street
Columbus, OH 43216-1618
(614) 644-2246

Oklahoma
Oklahoma Department of Labor
OSHA Division
4001 North Lincoln Boulevard
Oklahoma City, OK 73105-5212
(405) 528-1500

Oregon
Department of Insurance and Finance
Occupational Safety and Health Division
Labor and Industries Building
350 Winter Street, N.E., Room 430
Salem, OR 97310
(503) 378-3272

Pennsylvania
Indiana University of Pennsylvania
Safety Sciences Department
205 Uhler Hall
Indiana, PA 15705-1087
(412) 357-2561

Puerto Rico
Occupational Safety and Health Office
Department of Labor and Human Resources
505 Munoz Rivera Avenue, 21st Floor
Hato Rey, PR 00918
(787) 754-2188

Rhode Island
Division of Occupational Health
3 Capital Hill
Providence, RI 02908
(401) 277-2438

South Carolina
South Carolina Department of Labor, Licensing
 and Regulation
3600 Forest Drive
P.O. Box 11329
Columbia, SC 29204
(803) 896-4300

South Dakota
Engineering Extension
Onsite Technical Division
South Dakota State University, West Hall
907 Harvey Dunn Street
P.O. Box 510
Brookings, SD 57007
(605) 688-4101

Tennessee
OSHA Consultative Services Division
Tennessee Department of Labor
710 James Robertson Parkway, 3rd Floor
Nashville, TN 37243-0659
(615) 741-7036

Texas
Workers' Health and Safety Division
Workers' Compensation Commission
Southfield Building
4000 South I H 35
Austin, TX 78704
(512) 440-3834

Utah
State of Utah Labor Commission Workplace
 Safety and Health
Consultation Services
160 East 300 South
Salt Lake City, UT 84114-6650
(801) 530-7606

Vermont
Division of Occupational Safety and Health
Vermont Department of Labor and Industry
National Life Building, Drawer #20
Montpelier, VT 05602-3401
(802) 828-2765

Virginia
Virginia Department of Labor and Industry
Occupational Safety and Health Training
 and Consultation
13 South 13th Street
Richmond, VA 23219
(804) 786-6359

Virgin Islands
Division of Occupational Safety and Health
Virgin Islands Department of Labor
3021 Golden Rock
Christiansted
St. Croix, VI 00840
(809) 772-1315

Washington
Washington Department of Labor and Industries
Division of Industrial Safety and Health
P.O. Box 44643
Olympia, WA 98504
(360) 902-5638

West Virginia
West Virginia Department of Labor
Capitol Complex Building #3
1800 East Washington Street, Room 319
Charleston, WV 25305
(304) 558-7890

Wisconsin (Health)
Wisconsin Department of Health
 and Human Services
Division of Health
Section of Occupational Health
1414 East Washington Avenue, Room 112
Madison, WI 53703
(608) 266-8579

Wisconsin (Safety)
Wisconsin Department of Industry Labor
 and Human Relations
Bureau of Safety Inspections
401 Pilot Court, Suite C
Waukesha, WI 53188
(414) 521-5063

Wyoming
Wyoming Department of Employment
Workers' Safety and Compensation Division
Herschler Building, 2 East
122 West 25th Street, 2nd Floor
Cheyenne, WY 82002
(307) 777-7786

Other Relevant Addresses

Consultation Training Coordinator
OSHA Training Institute
1555 Training Institute
Des Plaines, IL 60018
(847) 297-4810

Laboratory Services Agreement
Wisconsin Occupational Health Lab
979 Jonathan Drive
Madison, WI 53713
(608) 263-8807

New York Public Sector Consultation Project
New York State Department of Labor
Building #12
State Building Campus
Albany, NY 12240
(518) 457-3518

Director of Consultation Support Services
University of Alabama
College of Continuing Studies
425 Martha Parham West
P.O. Box 870388
Tuscaloosa, AL 35487-0388
(205) 348-4585

OSHA Area Offices

US Department of Labor - OSHA
2047 Canyon Road - Todd Mall
Birmingham, AL 35216-1981
Telephone: (205) 731-1534

US Department of Labor - OSHA
3737 Government Boulevard, Suite 100
Mobile, AL 36693-4309
Telephone: (334) 441-6131

US Department of Labor - OSHA
301 W. Northern Lights Boulevard
Suite 407
Anchorage, AK 99503-7571
Telephone: (907) 271-5152

US Department of Labor - OSHA
3221 North 16th Street, Suite 100
Phoenix, AZ 85016
Telephone: (602) 640-2007

US Department of Labor - OSHA
425 West Capitol Avenue
Suite 450
Little Rock, AR 72201
Telephone: (501) 324-6291

US Department of Labor - OSHA
5675 Ruffin Road, Suite 330
San Diego, CA 92123
Telephone: (619) 557-2909

US Department of Labor - OSHA
1391 North Speer Boulevard
Suite 210
Denver, CO 80204-2552
Telephone: (303) 844-5285

US Department of Labor - OSHA
7935 E. Prentice Avenue, Suite 209
Englewood, CO 80111-2714
Telephone: (303) 843-4515

US Department of Labor - OSHA
Clark Building
Bridgeport, CT 06604
Telephone: (203) 579-5581

US Department of Labor - OSHA
Federal Office Building
450 Main Street, Room 613
Hartford, CT 06103
Telephone: (860) 240-3152

US Department of Labor - OSHA
1 Rodney Square, Suite 402
920 King Street
Wilmington, DE 19801
Telephone: (302) 573-6115

US Department of Labor - OSHA
Jacaranda Executive Court
8040 Peters Road
Building H-100
Fort Lauderdale, FL 33324
Telephone: (954) 424-0242

US Department of Labor - OSHA
Ribault Building
1851 Executive Center Drive
Suite 227
Jacksonville, FL 32207
Telephone: (904) 232-2895

US Department of Labor - OSHA
5807 Breckenridge Parkway
Suite A
Tampa, FL 33610-4249
Telephone: (813) 626-1177

US Department of Labor - OSHA
450 Mall Boulevard, Suite J
Savannah, GA 31406
Telephone: (912) 652-4393

US Department of Labor - OSHA
2400 Herodian Way, Suite 250
Smyrna, GA 30080-2968
Telephone: (770) 984-8700

US Department of Labor - OSHA
La Vista Perimeter Office Park
Building 7, Suite 110
Tucker, GA 30084-4154
Telephone: (770) 493-6644

US Department of Labor - OSHA
300 Ala Moana Boulevard, Suite 5-146
Honolulu, HI 96850
Telephone: (808) 541-2685

US Department of Labor - OSHA
1150 North Curtis Road
Suite 201
Boise, ID 83706-1234
Telephone: (208) 321-2960

US Department of Labor - OSHA
1600 167th Street, Suite 9
Calumet City, IL 60409
Telephone: (708) 891-3800

US Department of Labor - OSHA
2360 E. Devon Avenue
Suite 1010
Des Plaines, IL 60018
Telephone: (847) 803-4800

US Department of Labor - OSHA
344 Smoke Tree Business Park
North Aurora, IL 60542
Telephone: (630) 896-8700

US Department of Labor - OSHA
2918 West Willow Knolls Road
Peoria, IL 61614
Telephone: (309) 671-7033

US Department of Labor - OSHA
46 East Ohio Street, Room 422
Indianapolis, IN 46204
Telephone: (317) 226-7290

US Department of Labor - OSHA
210 Walnut Street, Room 815
Des Moines, IA 50309
Telephone: (515) 284-4794

US Department of Labor - OSHA
300 Epic Center
301 N. Main
Wichita, KS 67202
Telephone: (316) 269-6644

US Department of Labor - OSHA
John C. Watts Federal Building, Room 108
330 W. Broadway
Frankfort, KY 40601-7024
Telephone: (502) 227-2348

US Department of Labor - OSHA
9100 Bluebonnet Center Boulevard
Suite 201
Baton Rouge, LA 70809
Telephone: (504) 389-0474

US Department of Labor - OSHA
U.S. Federal Building
202 Harlow Street,
Room 211
Bangor, ME 04401
Telephone: (207) 941-8177

US Department of Labor - OSHA
300 West Pratt Street
Room 1110
Baltimore, MD 21201
Telephone: (410) 962-2840

US Department of Labor - OSHA
639 Granite Street, 4th Floor
Braintree, MA 02184
Telephone: (617) 565-6924

US Department of Labor - OSHA
Valley Office Park
13 Branch Street
Methuen, MA 01844
Telephone: (617) 565-8110

US Department of Labor - OSHA
1145 Main Street, Room 108
Springfield, MA 01103-1493
Telephone: (413) 785-0123

US Department of Labor - OSHA
801 South Waverly Road
Suite 306
Lansing, MI 48917-4200
Telephone: (517) 377-1892

US Department of Labor - OSHA
300 South 4th Street, Suite 1205
Minneapolis, MN 55401
Telephone: (612) 664-5460

US Department of Labor - OSHA
3780 I-55 North
Suite 210
Jackson, MS 39211-6323
Telephone: (601) 965-4606

US Department of Labor - OSHA
6200 Connecticut Avenue, Suite 100
Kansas City, MO 64120
Telephone: (816) 483-9531

US Department of Labor - OSHA
911 Washington Avenue
Room 420
St. Louis, MO 63101
Telephone: (314) 425-4249

US Department of Labor - OSHA
2900 4th Avenue North, Suite 303
Billings, MT 59101
Telephone: (406) 247-7494

US Department of Labor - OSHA
Overland Wolf Building, Room 100
6910 Pacific Street
Omaha, NE 68106
Telephone: (402) 221-3182

US Department of Labor - OSHA
705 North Plaza, Room 204
Carson City, NV 89701
Telephone: (702) 885-6963

US Department of Labor - OSHA
279 Pleasant Street, Suite 201
Concord, NH 03301
Telephone: (603) 225-1629

US Department of Labor - OSHA
1030 Saint Georges Avenue
Plaza 35, Suite 205
Avenel, NJ 07001
Telephone: (908) 750-3270

US Department of Labor - OSHA
500 Route 17 South, 2nd Floor
Hasbrouck Heights, NJ 07604
Telephone: (201) 288-1700

US Department of Labor - OSHA
Marlton Executive Park
701 Route 73 South, Suite 120
Marlton, NJ 08053
Telephone: (609) 757-5181

US Department of Labor - OSHA
299 Cherry Hill Road, Suite 304
Parsippany, NJ 07054
Telephone: (203) 263-1003

US Department of Labor - OSHA
505 Marquette Avenue, NW
Suite 820
Alburquerque, NM 87102
Telephone: (505) 248-5302

US Department of Labor - OSHA
401 New Karner Road
Suite 300
Albany, New York 12205-3809
Telephone: (518) 464-4338

US Department of Labor - OSHA
42-40 Bell Blvd. 5th Floor
Bayside, NY 11361
Telephone: (718) 279-9060

US Department of Labor - OSHA
5360 Genesee Street
Bowmansville, NY 14026
Telephone: (716) 684-3891

US Department of Labor - OSHA
6 World Trade Center, Room 881
New York, NY 10048
Telephone: (212) 466-2482

US Department of Labor - OSHA
3300 Vikery Road
Syracuse, NY 13212
Telephone: (315) 451-0808

US Department of Labor - OSHA
660 White Plaines Road
4th Floor
Tarrytown, NY 10591-5107
Telephone: (914) 524-7510

US Department of Labor - OSHA
990 Westbury Road
Westbury, NY 11590
Telephone: (516) 334-3344

US Department of Labor - OSHA
Century Station, Federal Building
300 Fayetteville Street Mall, Room 438
Raleigh, NC 27601-9998
Telephone: (919) 856-4770

US Department of Labor - OSHA
Federal Building, Room 348 3rd & Rosser
P.O. Box 2439
Bismarck, ND 58502
Telephone: (701) 250-4521

US Department of Labor - OSHA
36 Triangle Park Drive
Cincinnati, OH 45246
Telephone: (513) 841-4132

US Department of Labor - OSHA
Federal Office Building, Room 899
1240 East 9th Street
Cleveland, OH 44199
Telephone: (216) 522-3818

US Department of Labor - OSHA
Federal Office Building, Room 620
200 N. High Street
Columbus, OH 43215
Telephone: (614) 469-5582

US Department of Labor - OSHA
Federal Office Building, Room 734
234 North Summit Street
Toledo, OH 43604
Telephone: (419) 259-7542

US Department of Labor - OSHA
420 West Main, Suite 300
Oklahoma City, OK 73102
Telephone: (405) 231-5351

US Department of Labor - OSHA
1220 S.W. 3rd Avenue, Room 640
Portland, OR 97294
Telephone: (503) 326-2251

US Department of Labor - OSHA
850 N. 5th Street
Allentown, PA 18102
Telephone: (610) 776-0592

US Department of Labor - OSHA
3939 West Ridge Road
Suite B-12
Erie, PA 16506
Telephone: (814) 833-5758

US Department of Labor - OSHA
Progress Plaza
49 N. Progress Street
Harrisburg, PA 17109
Telephone: (717) 782-3902

US Department of Labor - OSHA
U.S. Custom House, Room 242
Second and Chestnut Street
Philadelphia, PA 19106
Telephone: (215) 597-4955

US Department of Labor - OSHA
Federal Building, Room 1428
1000 Liberty Avenue
Pittsburgh, PA 15222
Telephone: (412) 395-4903

US Department of Labor - OSHA
Stegmaier Building
7 North Wilksbarre Boulevard, Suite 410
Wilkes-Barre, PA 18701-18702
Telephone: (717) 826-6538

US Department of Labor - OSHA
BBV Plaza Building
1510 F.D. Roosevelt Avenue
Guaynabo, PR 00968
Telephone: (787) 277-1560

US Department of Labor - OSHA
380 Westminster Mall, Room 543
Providence, RI 02903
Telephone: (401) 528-4669

US Department of Labor - OSHA
1835 Assembly Street, Room 1468
Columbia, SC 29201-2453
Telephone: (803) 765-5904

US Department of Labor - OSHA
Green Hills Office Park
2002 Richard Jones Road
Suite C-205
Nashville, TN 37215-2809
Telephone: (615) 781-5423

US Department of Labor - OSHA
903 San Jacinto Boulevard
Suite 319
Austin, TX 78701
Telephone: (512) 916-5783

US Department of Labor - OSHA
Wilson Plaza
606 N. Carancahua, Suite 700
Corpus Christi, TX 78476
Telephone: (512) 888-3420

US Department of Labor - OSHA
8344 East R.L. Thornton Freeway
Suite 420
Dallas, TX 75228
Telephone: (214) 320-2400

US Department of Labor - OSHA
North Star 2 Building
8713 Airport Freeway, Suite 302
Fort Worth, TX 76180-7604
Telephone: (281) 428-2470

US Department of Labor - OSHA
17625 El Camino Real, Suite 400
Houston, TX 77060
Telephone: (281) 286-0583

US Department of Labor - OSHA
350 North Sam Houston Parkway
Suite 120
Houston, TX 77060
Telephone: (281) 591-2438

US Department of Labor - OSHA
Strum Thurman Federal Building, Room 804
1205 Texas Avenue
Lubbock, TX 79401
Telephone: (806) 472-7681

US Department of Labor - OSHA
1781 South 300 West
Salt Lake City, UT 84115-1802
Telephone: (801) 487-0073

US Department of Labor - OSHA
AFOB, Room 835
200 Granby Mall
Norfolk, VA 23510
Telephone: (757) 441-3820

US Department of Labor - OSHA
505 16th Avenue, N.E., Suite 302
Bellevue, WA 98004
Telephone: (206) 553-7520

US Department of Labor - OSHA
405 Capitol Street, Room 407
Charleston, WV 25301
Telephone: (304) 347-5937

US Department of Labor - OSHA
2618 North Ballard Road
Appleton, WI 54915-8664
Telephone: (920) 734-4521

US Department of Labor - OSHA
4802 East Broadway
Madison, WI 53716
Telephone: (608) 264-5388

US Department of Labor - OSHA
Henry S. Reuss Building
310 West Wisconsin Avenue, Suite 1180
Milwaukee, WI 53203
Telephone: (414) 297-3315

U.S. Department of Labor
Occupational Safety and Health Administration
Regional Offices

Region I
(CT,* MA, ME, NH, RI, VT*)
JFK Federal Building
Room E-340
Boston, MA 02203
Telephone: (617) 565-9860

Region II
(NJ, NY,* PR,* VI*)
201 Varick Street
Room 670
New York, NY 10014
Telephone: (212) 337-2378

Region III
(DC, DE, MD,* PA, VA,* WV)
Gateway Building, Suite 2100
3535 Market Street
Philadelphia, PA 19104
Telephone: (215) 596-1201

Region IV
(AL, FL, GA, KY,* MS, NC,* SC,* TN*)
Atlanta Federal Center
61 Forsyth Street SW, Room 6T50
Atlanta, GA 30303
Telephone: (404) 562-2300

Region V
(IL, IN,* MI,* MN,* OH, WI)
230 South Dearborn Street
Room 3244
Chicago, IL 60604
Telephone: (312) 353-2220

Region VI
(AR, LA, NM,* OK, TX)
525 Griffin Street
Room 602
Dallas, TX 75202
Telephone: (214) 767-4731

Region VII
(IA,* KS, MO, NE)
City Center Square
1100 Main Street, Suite 800
Kansas City, MO 64105
Telephone: (816) 426-5861

Region VIII
(CO, MT, ND, SD, UT,* WY*)
1999 Broadway, Suite 1690
Denver, CO 80202-5716
Telephone: (303) 844-1600

Region IX
(American Samoa, AZ,* CA,* Guam,
HI,* NV,* Trust Territories of the Pacific)
71 Stevenson Street
Room 420
San Francisco, CA 94105
Telephone: (415) 975-4310

Region X
(AK,* ID, OR,* WA*)
1111 Third Avenue
Suite 715
Seattle, WA 98101-3212
Telephone: (206) 553-5930

These states and territories operate their own OSHA-approved job safety and health programs (Connecticut and New York plans cover public employees only). States with approved programs must have a standard that is identical to, or at least as effective as, the federal standard.